BUY ON THE UPSIDE

BUY ON THE UPSIDE

Outsider Advice and
Encouragement for the Stock
Investor

Richard Howard and John Gordon

Copyright © 2004, 2005 by Richard Howard and John Gordon.

Library of Congress Number:		2005901577
ISBN:	Hardcover	1-4134-8781-5
	Softcover	1-4134-8780-7

All rights reserved. No part of this book may be reproduced or transmitted in any form or by any means, electronic or mechanical, including photocopying, recording, or by any information storage and retrieval system, without permission in writing from the copyright owner.

This book was printed in the United States of America.

To order additional copies of this book, contact:
Xlibris Corporation
1-888-795-4274
www.Xlibris.com
Orders@Xlibris.com
27212

Contents

PREFACE 7

CHAPTER 1: SNOW WHITE 11
Take Charge, Don't Wait for Your Prince to Come

CHAPTER 2: LITTLE RED RIDING HOOD 26
Learn to Live with the Big Bad Wolf

CHAPTER 3: GOLDILOCKS 38
Make Your Investment Strategy "Just Right"

CHAPTER 4: ALICE IN WONDERLAND 65
Confront and Understand the World You Are In

CHAPTER 5: BRER RABBIT 86
Contrive to Take Advantage of Adversity

CHAPTER 6: THE WIZARD OF OZ 102
You Are Not in Kansas Anymore: Principles for Success and Sound Sleep

CHAPTER 7: THE FOX AND THE HEDGEHOG 114
You Need to Know Both One Big Thing and Many Small Ones: A Checklist for Takeoff as a Retail Investor

ENDNOTES 119
Web Site Companion to This Book: *www.buyupside.com*

INDEX 121

PREFACE

We are both retail investors. One of us, Howard, has supported himself solely by investing in stocks for twelve years. We both are fallen-away academics with PhDs (Gordon was a professor and dean at Yale; Howard was on the faculty and head of computing at Clark University). But neither of us has formally studied finance, economics, or the stock market beyond the usual poorly comprehended undergraduate courses. Howard's doctorate is in forestry, and Gordon's is in the physiology and biochemistry of trees. We both have undergraduate degrees in forestry, a profession that, if nothing else, prepares one for the long view. But neither of us is from, of, or at all connected to Wall Street.

This is both a modest admission and a boast. We presume to think that there are other people like us who would enjoy an outsider's view of the retail investment process and what we have come to call the "Wall Street Buy Machine."

Some of what we have to say you will have heard before in some form. But we think our often contrarian perspective on such chestnuts as "buy and hold," "diversify," and "don't time the market," gained through painful experience, will be interesting and useful. Some other things are new. We have developed new quantitative techniques that are particularly helpful to people who want to buckle down and learn enough to be at least as serious about investing as Ivy Leaguers are about squash. These quantitative indicators are not magic identifiers of stock or market tops and bottoms, nor do they give automatic buy-and-sell signals. But they can help you make important decisions.

What they do is provide retail investors (those of us who invest but are not Wall Street professionals) with a solid foundation for what academics call a "decision support system" (DSS). Despite having a rather awkward name, DSS embodies a key concept. No matter how much information you have, actual decisions should be made inside the human brain, still the best integrator of disparate facts. No one but you knows what you really want to do, and often, if you are like us, even you don't know until the time comes to decide something. The DSS tracks information and bundles it into logical and useful options that are ready when you are. That is this book: a simple and understandable DSS for the retail investor in stocks.

Now both in our sixties, we sometimes have trouble remembering things. So we have structured our book around stories that we all remember because they were drilled into us in childhood. The enduring children's tales, often inaccurately called "fairy stories," endure for a reason. Each teaches at least one life lesson, or provides a useful perspective on how to deal with particular life situations, or both. We hope that by keying our advice and perspective to some of these we make them easier to remember and clearer. There is so much advice and information about the stock market aimed at the retail investor that we think the forest is often missed because of the proliferation of trees (sorry, but we said we were foresters).

For example, the eventual profit (or loss) from things bought to be sold again, most often is determined at the outset by their purchase price. This is true of stocks, bonds, real estate, commodities, horses, timber, and anything else we can think of. A couple of extreme stock purchase examples illustrate this. If you bought the Dow at its peak in 1929, you next came up for air (with a positive gain) in 1954. If you bought NASDAQ at its peak in 2000, you are still under water and probably will be for some time to come. On the other hand, if you bought the Dow at its 1932 low, you have seen money ahead every day since then.

Thus, we think most bad investments are the result of moving too quickly to pay too much. But the stock market has a spirited reply, which poses a hellish problem. How do you know, at any given time, what is too much? One answer is that you can't, or at least that it is so hard as to make trying unproductive. This is the "random walk" notion, made famous by Professor Burton Malkiel in his excellent best-seller *A Random Walk on Wall Street*.[1] Malkiel shows that experts don't pick stocks any better than "a bare-assed ape throwing darts." We tend to agree unless you want to spend some real effort on your investment life. But we think that if you do, you can beat the ape going away, at least in relation to your own goals.

But first, you need to get the fundamentals right and remember to use them in every investment decision. Given that you are an individual with unique goals, there are no "no-brainer" decisions. Second, you need to decide how aggressive you want to be. If you are willing to work hard, there are tools of fundamental (looking at the details of company performance) and technical (looking at the behavior of the markets) analysis to help you make better market decisions. Finally, you need to continually put investment decisions in the context of your life. How much time can or will you devote to investing compared with other activities? If you are willing to devote an hour each day to stocks, read on and prosper. Or just read on. At least you will know for sure what you are missing. And be sure to visit this book's companion Web site, www.*buyupside.com*. It contains a wealth of additional information and it's free.

CHAPTER 1

Snow White

> *Whether you achieve outstanding results will depend on the effort and intellect you apply to your investments, as well as on the amplitudes of stock-market folly that prevail during your investing career.*
>
> —Warren E. Buffett, preface to *The Intelligent Investor* by Benjamin Graham[2]

Snow White waited for her prince to come, and almost wound up dead. Don't wait for your prince to come. To make money in the stock market, you need to be proactive. This means being motivated, setting goals, making plans, studying the stock world, and most of all, taking responsibility for your investment decisions. As classroom veterans, we think personal example is often the best teaching tool. In this chapter, we talk basics about stocks and bonds, and Richard Howard tells about his investor's journey to confidence, focus, and realism. But first, we review briefly the basics of stocks for stock market beginners. If you are not one, skip to the next section. Whether you are a beginner or a more experienced investor, begin now to become familiar with the Web site *www.buyupside.com*. It contains a huge range of data and advice on everything from sector funds to example portfolios. Also, it explains two important analytical tools for more advanced investors, the Complete Trading Model (CTM) and the Price Direction Indicator (PDI). These tools, developed by Richard Howard, are enormously helpful in identifying market trends and are particularly useful for analyzing and trading cyclical stocks. And it is free.

What Is a "Stock"?

When you buy stock (we are talking about what are technically called common stocks) you are buying "shares" of a company. The price of an individual unit (share) of a stock multiplied by the number of shares the company has sold ("shares outstanding") is one measure of the value of the company, and is call "market capitalization." By buying shares, you become an owner of the company that issues the stock. You are entitled to attend annual meetings, vote on the selection of the board of directors, and other important matters and receive dividends, which may be in the form of cash or additional shares of stock. You may obtain a paper stock certificate as proof of ownership or record your shares at your broker's firm. You may buy and sell shares at anytime; thus you can buy stocks and hold them until you retire or you can actively trade stocks by the minute.

A share of a well-managed company has the potential for price appreciation so you can make a profit on your investment, a compelling reason to buy a stock. If, however, the stock price falls you can lose money. Before you purchase any stock, be sure to learn about the company. Research its products, quality of management, and future profit growth prospects. This is called "fundamental analysis."

Some companies pay dividends to shareholders from current or accumulated profits. A shareholder receives a dividend for each share owned. For example, if a company pays a $1.20 annual dividend, a shareholder with two hundred shares receives $240 for the year. A dividend is usually paid every three months so the quarterly dividend is $60 for this example. For an investor, who wants dollar income, a dividend-paying stock may be the answer.

A company issues stock to receive money from the sale of its stock. The number of shares owned by shareholders is called the shares outstanding. The total value of a company can be measured by multiplying the shares outstanding by the current price of the stock. This amount is called the market capitalization. For example, a stock with one hundred million shares outstanding selling at $50 per share has a market capitalization of $5 billion.

A company may choose to split its stock when the price becomes so high that some investors regard it as too expensive to purchase. Upon splitting, the number of shares that you own increases according to the magnitude of the split. But the value of your shares remains unchanged because the price per share is adjusted accordingly. Assume you own one hundred shares of a $50 stock that splits two for one. This means you will now own two hundred shares but the price of the stock is reduced to $25. So the value of your shares is still $5,000 after the spilt.

Occasionally a company with a very low-priced stock will execute a reverse split, which decreases the number of shares that you own but increases the stock price. A company would do a reverse split because some investors will not purchase low-priced stocks. For example, a five for one reverse split means one hundred shares become twenty and a $2 stock price becomes $10. The total value of your shares is unchanged.

If a company is liquidated, the stock you own is usually worthless and you will lose your entire investment. Other creditors are paid before the owners of common stock. But if you buy the stock of a well-established, well-managed company, the likelihood of the stock going to zero is remote.

Howard's Story

I "retired" from Digital Equipment Corporation in June 1993 at age fifty-three. I was sick of the corporate world of deadlines, performance reviews, and action items; uncertainty about layoffs and budget cuts; inept management, lack of corporate direction, and waste of resources; endless meetings resulting in nothing; working on projects that were cancelled or resulted in no profitable revenue; empire building, management by committee and consensus, team building, departmental and corporate reorganizations. In short, I was sick of going to work.

Each morning as I parked my car in the Digital lot and got out to head for the building, the most important question I asked myself was "How soon can I leave work today?" I needed a change.

On May 25, 1993, I arrived at the office around 9 a.m. and checked my e-mail as usual. The only message was from my boss asking me to call him as soon as possible. I called him to learn that the funding for my pet project had been eliminated just four weeks after approval. In fact, I composed an e-mail to my boss, his boss, and his boss's boss stating that, due to the funding cut, "I had no more contributions to make to Digital." I sent the e-mail and started to clean out my office. After an hour or so I left for home. After fifteen years at Digital, I was going to be free!

My Wife's Reaction

When my wife arrived home from her job late that afternoon, she knew something was up when I greeted her at the front door with a big hug and said, "I quit." "What?" she replied. And then she asked, "What are you going to do after that?" For the last three years I had not been happy at work and I had been asking myself that very question. "What would I do if I didn't work at Digital?" I knew I needed an income so I couldn't just quit and do nothing. Since 1982 I had dabbled in the stock market. In 1987, just after the market crash, I began to put money into the market regularly. After surviving the crash, I realized I had the stomach for the inevitable ups and downs that stocks deliver so I decided to become an active investor. With money I earned from a part-time teaching job, I stashed cash in a money-market account. This pile would become instrumental in my post-Digital plan. We spent the evening discussing our plans and in the end we were both in complete agreement. **I would leave the corporate world and pursue full-time trading in the stock market. Her support was crucial to my plan.** *Note: It is important to identify and record your initial commitment to constructing a system for investment. You may not make as radical a break with the past* as Howard did (few will, although perhaps more should). Nevertheless, becoming an informed retail investor is serious business, and infinitely dangerous if not pursued diligently once the commitment is made. Despite the many disclaimers from Wall Street mavens, investing in stocks is a form of gambling. The investor makes bets, and some pay off and some don't. You wouldn't dream of playing poker with professional gamblers without serious study of and experience in the game (we hope). In the stock market, you are playing against many, rather than a few, people. As in poker, some people win fairly consistently regardless of the cards they are dealt. Skill does count. Unlike poker, in the stock market your most determined opponents often claim to be on your side. This is what we call the "Wall Street Buy Machine." Basically, this means that the professionals connected to the market and accessible to most retail investors make money as the volume and fees of stock purchases and sales rise. They collect these fees whether you make money or not. Their interest then is in trading, when yours is in making money. Sometimes these interests align but often they don't. Unless you make the commitment enough to know when your and, say, your broker's interests align, you will have a tough time as a retail investor.

The Layoff

I was formally terminated at Digital on June 30, 1993. I received a generous severance package of six months' salary and an extension on a previously issued options grant of five hundred shares of Digital stock, which eventually terminated as worthless. Digital stock plummeted and the subsequent purchase by Compaq didn't revive the stock.

The severance money bought me time to construct a plan to generate income. I knew I was not going back to work in high tech or teaching and had decided to trade stocks to earn my living. I was fifty-three years old and had ten years of experience casually buying and selling stocks. I had $113,000 in cash saved from the part-time teaching job and other stocks in an IRA account and more stocks in a long-term buy-and-hold dividend reinvestment program. **The first task I had was to inventory and organize this smattering of stocks and cash.** *Note: This is the first step in constructing your investment decision support system. Make an absolutely accurate assessment of what you have, and what you need. This goes beyond constructing the usual "net worth" sheet and a detailed budget. You need to know what specific portions of your resources you can risk in the stock market, how much money you can save, and what needs to be set aside for "contingencies," those unexpected happenings that cost money. Although the core of our message is that everyone is different and thus everyone's decision support system for stocks is different, we also think that some general conditions are particularly consistent with becoming a successful investor.* **Three qualities—confidence, focus, and realism—determine investing success.** *Your personal financial condition underpins these. We suggest that you should:*

- *assure that the place you live in is secure, with rent or a mortgage payment that is well within your means. If you are a homeowner, paying off your mortgage is usually a good investment and substantial equity in a home is a confidence builder. If you have home equity we strongly recommend you don't use it to buy stocks;*
- *pay off credit card debt. Few investments make 10 to 20 percent over the long term, and that is what you usually make by paying off the card balances. If you are distracted*

by heavy debts, you are unlikely to achieve the focus you need to do well in the stock market;
- *make sure you are estimating your future income and expenses as realistically as possible, and be conservative in your income estimates. Have a contingency cash fund of at least two months normal income. Only through this degree of realism will you know what you can risk in the market.*

The Three-pile Plan

During the summer of 1993, I developed my plan. I knew I could start receiving my Digital retirement in 1995 when I turned fifty-five. Also, I decided to start my Social Security at age sixty-two, which would be in 2002. Therefore, I needed to generate cash for my expenses from 1993 to 2002.

I decided to use the $113,000 cash pile as my cash-register account. Out of that pile, I would draw money for monthly expenses and trading money.

The second pile, the stocks in dividend reinvestment plans, would be available if I ran out of money in the first pile. My intent was not to use money from the second pile unless absolutely necessary.

The third pile, the IRA, would be available at no penalty when I turned fifty-nine and a half, but I didn't want to touch the IRA until after that. I would trade in this account but not use it for immediate income needs. *Note: This plan would not work for everyone, but everyone should have a realistic plan. For many, Howard's first "pile" will be the income from a job, and the portion of this that can be allocated to trading, rather than monthly expenses, is critical to know.* His second pile, stocks in dividend reinvestment plans, should be, we think, a feature of everyone's stock investment strategy. Begun early and watched carefully, these stocks can be the core and low-maintenance value generator for the construction of wealth. We treat these in more detail in a subsequent chapter. The third pile, a tax-sheltered retirement account, should also be a feature of everyone's approach to investing. Gains that accrue tax free obviously build faster than those that don't. Beyond that, knowing that you are making your retirement more secure is a terrific confidence builder. We also examine retirement planning in some detail in a later chapter.

Start of Trading

I started trading stocks in June 1993 while I was still finalizing the three-pile strategy. I worked with my broker, a vice president with a nationally known full-service brokerage house. In the parlance of the brokerage professional I was called a retail client or retail investor. I had had an account with my broker since 1982. I knew him well and liked to work with him. I also knew he had much more experience than I and that I could learn a lot from him.

I surmised I could do better with his help than striking out on my own so I was willing to pay full commissions because I trusted his suggestions and judgment. Soon he discounted the commissions because of my frequent trading. I never considered that the commissions I was paying were a significant factor in my trading decisions. If I made money, I made money. He and I worked closely as a team and if we did well we both would benefit.

Finally, I reasoned that when you have dental problems, you go to a dentist. You can't drill your own teeth. Same with your investing decisions. Get advice from a professional you can trust. Don't make all these important investment decisions by yourself when you're learning how to trade. By the way, in 1996, I opened an account with an online discount broker. The first time I attempted to access my account, the online site was down. I never used it again. I learned the interaction with my broker was far more beneficial than the savings on commissions from a discount broker. *Note: The least reason for having a broker is to execute trades. Perhaps the right analogy for having access to a broker you know, trust, and can talk with is the intelligence community. Like the intelligence community, you can learn a lot about stocks and mutual funds from remote observation. Web sites, TV networks, newsletters, stock and fund rating concerns, books, magazines, and your own passive observations all can provide valuable information to use in stock investing. But as in the intelligence community, there is no substitute for "humint," the ability to get information from and to discuss strategy with people you trust. Finding the right broker and building the right relationship for you with her is a key to being a successful "independent" investor. We discuss this in more detail in the next chapter.*

Trading Activities

1993, 1994, and 1995 were very active trading years. I was not a day trader—a person sitting at a computer, trading minute by minute. I wanted to have a life outside the stock market. I made a few trades each month. I only bought individual stocks long. I went short once, lost money in a few days, covered the short position, and never again shorted a stock. I rarely traded options and never bought on margin.

My strategy was simple: take quick profits, avoid large losses by taking small losses. Never get into a situation that could lead to a catastrophic loss. Always have cash on hand for the next trade.

I had a very compelling motivation. If I failed to get it right, I would have to go back to a regular job in the real world. After a taste of freedom and independence, the last thing I wanted was a real job and to report to a boss every day. *Note: The realism of having to make a living at stock trading provided Howard both an urgent motivation and a desire to be careful. Also, partially because of these, he started carefully with basic trading of "long" positions in stocks without using borrowed or margin money. Using the more esoteric forms of stock trading should come rather far up the learning curve, and maybe never to most retail investors who have day jobs.*

Making My Own Decisions
In the fall of 1994, I loaded up on a retail store stock that I read about in a newsletter I subscribed to. The letter writer touted the stock and I went along with his recommendation. I visited one of their retail stores during the Christmas-buying season to get a feel for the operation. I didn't like the store or its merchandise. After Christmas, the store reported lower than expected same-store sales and the stock fell. I sold the stock before it plummeted. The company eventually went out of business and the stock went to zero.

After that experience, I cancelled the newsletter because the writer would tell you when to buy but never when to sell. That was my "near death experience" in my trading career and I didn't like the feeling. But I did learn a powerful lesson, which ultimately saved my trading career: **RELY ON YOUR OWN JUDGMENT.**

You can listen to other people's recommendations, but don't blindly accept them. From that time forward I decided to make my own decisions. I'll stand or fall on my own. If I goof, it's my error. If I succeed, I can thank someone else for their input and recommendations, but I'll thank myself for the good luck. *Note: Here lies the essence of the DSS approach. Gather all the support for your decisions you can. The more systematically you do this, and the more carefully you record the results, the better. But treat each decision as what scientists call a hypothesis. A hypothesis is an educated guess, which, in the best instance, does two things. First, it specifies a future outcome that can be verified or tested. Second, it says why you would expect the prediction to come true. The use of hypotheses advances science because they open every new idea to careful and skeptical scrutiny. So it should be with your stock-trading decisions. Before executing, you should treat the proposed trade as a hypothesis and try to disprove it. What are the reasons that it might not succeed? If these seem more compelling than the information supporting the trade, discard the hypothesis; that is, don't make the trade.*

Admitting Mistakes

I quickly learned that I had to admit I had made a mistake when a trade went bad. In 1994 I bought stocks of copper and nickel producers, thinking they would bounce up. I knew commodity stocks such as these were extremely volatile but I was willing to take the chance. Shortly after I bought the stocks, they started to move down. I was down about 10 percent when I sold all my shares. They continued down another 30 percent. I lost money on the trades but I avoided a disaster by recognizing that I was wrong about the direction of the price movement. I got out and had the money available for another trade.

When you accept how unexpectedly and rapidly stocks can turn down, you quickly learn methods to preserve your trading capital. I never used formal stop losses (shares are sold automatically at a predetermined price). But rather, I watched the stocks daily and after the confirmation of bad news and a drop in the price, I simply sold as quickly as possible. If the stock bounced back after I sold it, that was fine because I met my objective of preserving my money. I learned not to beat myself up when stocks moved up immediately after I sold them. When I learned that each trade was a new learning experience, much of the emotional burden was lifted. I began to enjoy trading because my winners outnumbered my losers. Obviously, I lucked out in the timing of my trading career. In the 1990s the market kept rising and covered up a lot up of my trading mistakes. I could make a bad trade, then almost immediately make money on another trade. If I'd been in a full-fledged bear market, I wonder if I would have survived. In bull markets you can get fooled into thinking your success is because of your skill, but in reality it might be due in large part to luck. The book *Fooled by Randomness* by N. N. Tales[3] discusses in detail the notion of luck versus skill. I like to think my trading success was mostly from skill, but I recognize luck played a major role. But this luck also taught me the wisdom of the "buy on the upside" philosophy and led me to work to quantify how to identify the upside. *Note: Above, we talked about hypothesis testing. The real test occurs after the trade. This is not useful for the trade in question, but can speak volumes about the future. Perhaps the most important lesson in investing after the one that says "buy at the right price" is "don't ride stocks down," unless you are committed to an absolute buy-and-hold strategy (for which there are some valid reasons for some people and stocks). As it turns out, this second lesson transformed into quantitative tools for supporting stock decisions that have considerable accuracy. We discuss these in the chapter on the complete trading model (CTM) and the price direction indicator (PDI). The capsule lesson is "buy on the upside," hence the name of this book.*

The Future

Sometimes I think that if I had continued to work until age sixty-two, I would have saved and invested a lot more money and my retirement accounts would be worth much more than they are today. They probably would be, but what of it? I don't need the extra money. I have enough money for my lifetime and then some. I decided some time ago that when the pile gets large enough, it doesn't have to be any larger. *Note: It is important to understand that Howard identified the "bubble" in the stock market while most others were denying that a bubble existed, or at least were not sure. He did this not through a lucky guess, but by carefully assessing all the evidence available to him. Indeed, this experience was* the beginning of the analytical work that resulted in the CTM. He acted on this advice in 1999 (and convinced me, Gordon, against my natural optimism, also to do so) and we saved what was to us a lot of money. Or rather, we made a lot of money, because we moved to cash or bonds after the major run up in stock prices well before the major decline, the bursting of the bubble. As it turned out, we could have gone to "cash" even a couple of years earlier and still done respectably well. The point here is to not be afraid to go to cash when conditions indicate you should as we discuss in a later chapter. Another important lesson is to not let greed trump realism. Making money is a good thing if it helps you achieve your life goals. It can also provide the stimulus and fun of competition and risk taking. But taken too far it can ruin your judgment and render your decision support system useless. How to develop the confidence, focus, and realism to identify and use the upside forms the rest of this book.

CHAPTER 2

Little Red Riding Hood

The Wall Street Buy Machine plays the Big Bad Wolf to the beginning investor's Little Red Riding Hood by seeming benign and even helpful, while having a concealed desire to eat the contents of your basket.

According to the National Association of Securities Dealers (NASD), July 2003,[4] there are 660,904 registered securities representatives working in 94,204 offices for 5,331 brokerage firms in the United States. By comparison, the Bureau of Labor Statistics[5] estimated that dentists numbered 152,000, or about one quarter the number of securities professionals. Everyone has (or has had) teeth, but only about half of us invest in stocks. Why are there so many brokers? The answer is simple: to entice you to buy stocks, bonds, mutual funds, and other investments.

You see the "Wall Street Buy Machine" everywhere. For instance, financial programs on TV and radio routinely tout stocks. Brokerage houses promote their lists of favorite stocks to buy. Popular financial magazines publish article after article about hot stocks and what you should buy. Seductive brochures accompany your monthly or quarterly mutual fund or brokerage account statements, espousing the merits of owning stocks. Brokers, trying to earn a living from sales commissions, routinely call you to hawk the latest "great stock" or fund. After you pay for a subscription, a newsletter writer provides lists of stocks you must own now. Stock mutual funds ads tell you how much money you can make in the long run. The federal government gives you tax breaks to maintain a retirement account that presumably contains stocks. And your employer sets up plans so you can buy stocks for your retirement account. The *Machine* tells us to buy stocks at anytime at any price. We retail investors are confronted by a withering campaign of buy, buy, buy.

Making Money Is Not Easy

Near the peak of the 1990s bull market, investors, with lots of encouragement from Wall Street, threw money at stocks and many made large profits. People became accustomed to large gains and expected them to continue. They didn't realize that stocks can't go up forever because at some point everyone who wanted to buy at a higher price has done so. In the absence of new buyers and any bad or unexpected news, the sellers step in and the prices begin to drop. The mantra of investing in the late 1990s was that it was easy to make money in stocks: just about anybody with half a brain and a few thousand dollars to invest could hit the jackpot. The prolonged bull market let investors think that making money was easy. Ever-increasing prices masked basic investing mistakes like paying too much, buying a company that has no viable business plan (many Internet stocks), failure to sell a stock after making a handsome profit, loading up on the stocks in the same hot sector, and believing all the media and Wall Street hype saying "it's different this time." Remember the "New Economy"?

The bursting of the NASDAQ bubble in 2000 changed these views of investing. The illusion that investing in the stock market is a trivial pursuit ended in March 2000.

Mutual Fund Lessons

According to John Bogle,[6] mutual fund industry assets have grown from $2 billion in 1949 to $6.5 trillion at the beginning of 2004. The total number of funds (stock, bond, and money market) is now about 8,300. Stock funds total 4,800, a number not much smaller than the 5,700 stocks included in the Wilshire 5000, the broadest index of U.S.-based equities. Obviously, the industry knows how to sell funds to the public. From 1998 to 2000, the top of the 1982-2000 bull market, investors were sold $555 billion of mostly speculative stock funds.

According to *Forbes* magazine,[7] seventy-one new-technology mutual funds were offered in 2000. As the market collapsed in 2000, much of that new money simply evaporated. But the commissions and fees did not. Each of these funds needs money to pay its expenses that include salaries, wages, commissions and bonuses, computers to keep track of your account, postage to mail statements and reports, and marketing and advertising to programs to promote the funds.

To cover these and other expenses, a mutual fund charges an annual fee which usually runs from 1 to 3 percent of the total assets under management. So if you own a fund worth $10,000, your annual charge is $100 for a 1 percent fee. The $100 doesn't seem like much but when you compute the sum of the fees for all funds sold by the industry, the total amount is enormous. For example, given mutual fund assets were $6.5 trillion and the cost of ownership was 1.28 percent (according to the Investment Company Institute[8]) income to mutual fund managers would be **$83.2 billion** (1.28 percent times $6.5 trillion). And the funds take in these fees whether the fund's value is going down or going up.

The long-term performance of the mutual-fund industry demonstrates that making money in the stock market is difficult. Eighty-five percent of all mutual funds do worse than the S&P 500.[9] This means that the highly motivated, well-trained, and educated group of professional managers usually can't beat a broad measure of market performance. For example, if the S&P 500 is up 12 percent in a year, only 15 percent of all mutual funds would have returned 12 percent or better for that year. As hard as they try to select the best performing stocks, they can't consistently beat the overall market. This suggests that these managers are doing something fundamentally wrong or that stock selection is not an easy task or both.

What Is the Long-term?

Many Wall Street sages tell us that buy-and-hold is the correct strategy for long-term investors. They cite historical stock market returns of 6-8 percent per year for the past one hundred years.[10] These rates of return are misleading because they represent averages. They don't tell us about the strings of years when the market is down, or flat. The averages smooth out these wrinkles in the market and make it look like the long-term performance is ever upward. In reality, even though the "long-term" trend is up, short-term returns vary greatly, and from losses to gains.

A major problem for individual investors is that their definition of "long term" is different from the definition of "long term" for the market, which essentially is forever. People, on the other hand, usually have a relatively brief period of being invested in the market. Most people who invest start in their forties and stop adding new money at retirement when they start to withdraw money. This means the long-term view for an individual is a few decades, not one hundred plus years. When "your" years occur in relation to market, and individual stock performance can determine almost completely whether you succeed or fail.

Thus, while a buy-and-hold strategy works for a long period of increasing prices, it may not ensure profits in the time frame of individual investors. For the investor in a multiyear period of price declines or flat price patterns, a buy-and-hold strategy may lead to a significant decrease in net worth. One clear resultant guideline is to invest over as long a period as possible. Start young and stay at it. Specific examples and advice on "buy and hold" are found in chapter 4.

Also, the long-term averages are based on overall market performance, which consists of thirty stocks for the DJIA and five hundred stocks for the S&P 500. Few investors own five hundred stocks. Because the performance of portfolios with fewer stocks tends to be more volatile than portfolios with more stocks, individual investors' returns will be more volatile than market performance suggests. Therefore, some investors will beat the market by a substantial amount and some will do significantly worse than the market.

Because each investor has unique goals and a unique investing style, each has a unique investing track record. No two investors will have the same outcomes. Some will do well and others will not.

What all this means is that you should be as wary of the Wall Street Buy Machine as you would be of an actual wolf. Its experience, marketing savvy, financial resources, and huge sales force make it a formidable foe. Before you buy or sell, complete your own due diligence to ensure that you are not seduced or devoured.

Beware of Professional Buy-and-sell Recommendations

Bashing stock analysts' recommendations has become fashionable since the stock market bubble burst in 2000. The following chart shows there is legitimate justification to continue.

Figure 1. KLIC price upgrades and downgrades, 1998-2004.

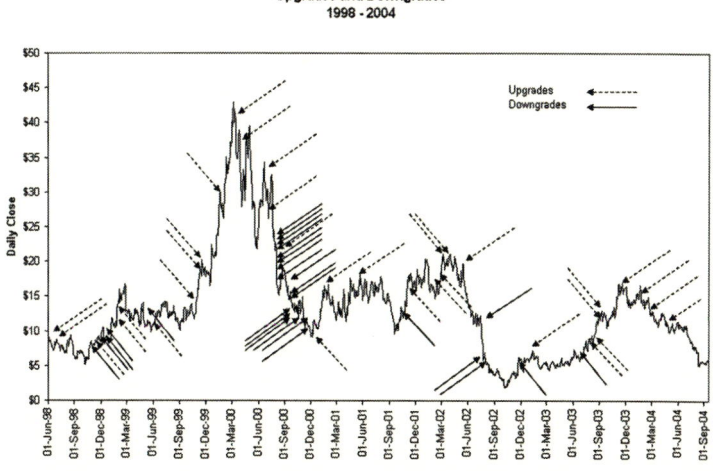

For example, since May 1998, analysts have made sixty-three upgrade (buy) and downgrade (sell) recommendations for Kulicke & Soffa (KLIC), a semiconductor equipment maker (Figure 1). The chart of recommendations and closing prices (see Yahoo! Finance for the list of upgrades and downgrades[11]) shows a pattern of buy-high, sell-low recommendations.

The cluster of downgrades in the summer and fall of 2000 is especially striking. Rather than tell you to sell at high prices as KLIC peaked in the mid $40 range, analysts waited until the stock tumbled 40 percent or more to tell you to sell. The same sell-low pattern is evident in the summer and fall of 2002. For the current cycle, analysts are telling us the buy on the downside after the stock peaked in November 2003. There were some good buy calls on the upside but most recommendations told us to buy near the top, to buy on the downside, or to sell low.

During the period from April 1, 2002, to April 16, 2004, analysts made fourteen upgrade (buy) and downgrade (sell) recommendations of which eleven produced unprofitable trades. If you had followed their recommendations and invested $14,000 ($1,000 per recommendation), you would have ended up with $10,018.06—a loss of 39.75 percent. Your largest single loss was 74.84 percent and your best single gain was 25 percent (buy recommendations without a corresponding sell recommendation were evaluated using the April 16, 2004, closing price of $10.95). During this period, KLIC fell from $21.15 to $1.95 and then rose a spectacular 767 percent to $16.9. So even when the stock price rose over eightfold ($1.95 to $16.9) the best analyst pick was a gain of only 25 percent. To summarize, eleven of the fourteen recommendations were unprofitable, with an almost 40 percent loss averaged across all recommendations.

How did professional analysts from eight well-known brokerage and research firms give such horrific, amateurish advice? Simply put: they violated many sound buy-and-sell principles. They bought on the downside and they bought on the upside near the top. And they sold near the bottom.

The next time you're tempted to buy or sell based on analysts' recommendations remember this data.

Choosing and Managing Your Broker

All the foregoing cautionary information doesn't imply you can or should invest without help, including "Wall Street" help. Investors who work effectively with their broker do better than those who don't. Your broker is usually an essential part of your stock decision support system, but she almost always identifies strongly with the Big Bad Wolf. Why? Consider what brokers do for a living. Their job description, as defined by the Bureau of Labor Statistics,[12] includes the following paragraph: "The most important part of a sales representative's job is finding clients and building a customer base. Thus, beginning securities and commodities sales agents spend much of their time searching for customers, relying heavily on telephone solicitation." So when a broker calls, remember she must be paid, and her sales commissions will come from your pocket when you buy or sell.

Thus it is extremely important to choose your broker carefully and to treat her respectfully but with caution. A good overall tactic for broker management is to gather independent information regarding each decision the broker recommends. Thoroughly check each recommendation your broker makes and discuss your information and hers until any differences are resolved to your satisfaction. A better broker management technique is to (think of General Patton) stay on the offensive. Form your own recommendations and then try them on your broker, encouraging her to be a "friendly adversary." If she can't talk you out of it, go ahead. Your best default position, in the face of really conflicting evidence, is to not buy or sell. In any event, treat your broker as a key part of your decision support system, but don't let your broker make decisions for you.

The most important criterion for choosing a broker is to find one that is compatible with you in investing style, personality, and accessibility. You must be able to talk freely and honestly with your broker, and you must work with one long enough so that mutual trust and respect are established. The broker must be willing to spend time with you, and must understand your goals and investing style. For some people, these stringent criteria may only be met by a fee-for-service financial advisor.

Are You a Committed Investor?

See if you think the investors quoted below have the commitment and knowledge needed to produce "historic returns" by investing in stocks. Then ask yourself, "Do I want to be like them?" Only serious self-knowledge can be the basis for commitment to trading stocks (or anything else).

BUY ON THE UPSIDE

(from *Money,* September 2002[13])

Woman, 52
Bought shares in:
Ralston Purina because the company is based in her hometown; Gillette because her three sons swear by the Mach 3 razor; Wells Fargo because her friend Susie loved working there. She'd already purchased shares of Martha Stewart's company: "I'd once met Martha and her hands weren't smooth and beautiful and I thought, 'She must actually do the work.'"

Her sort of "gut feeling" all too often overrides careful, committed thought and analysis for many investors. Sometimes it works, but more often not.

Man, 52
Has 100 percent of his retirement account in company stock. "I have great confidence in the company," he says. Note: the company is Procter & Gamble.

Confidence does not replace analysis, and no retirement account should depend on one stock.

Woman, age not given
"I entered the market right as tech stocks were peaking in 1999. For a short window, you didn't have to know anything to feel like you could do anything. They'd shoot up in a day. I'd just buy more."

The "bubble" of the '90s created many stock-picking geniuses on the way up. Many continued to buy on the downside when the bubble broke.

Woman, 38; man, 42
"We bought Cisco, Oracle, and all the hot stocks touted by analysts. We also had some small caps and technical stuff—we were practically day trading."

Most inexperienced day traders lose money.

Man, 43
"My goal is to match historic market return of 10 percent to 11 percent." Note: He owns eleven mutual funds

The committed investor gets facts straight. Historic returns most often quoted are more likely 6 to 8 percent, and there is probably no valid reason to own eleven mutual funds.

Man, 28
Eventually, he says, he'd like to purchase rental properties: "I want to try that and see how it goes."

The committed investor would want to know in detail about the business of investing in rental properties before "seeing how it goes."

Woman, 44; man, 52
Kim had been managing their six-figure portfolio but its size and changing market had gotten to be too much for her. So last year the couple decided to hire a financial planner. Kim, happy to have the burden off her shoulders, says the planner calculates that they have a 98 percent probability of reaching their retirement goals. Now, she says, "I feel more confident."

A good financial planner or a broker is a good thing, but they are not a substitute for commitment.

Only commitment backed by the willingness to spend time working hard will allow you to develop the confidence, focus, and realism to be a successful retail investor.

CHAPTER 3

Goldilocks

Goldilocks got the better of the bears and was good at finding things that were "just right." In the same way, you should continually balance your investments and their performance against your goals. Only you can know completely what those are. Thus, as we will continue to repeat, information helps you make decisions, it doesn't make decisions for you. Your goals are unique to your situation, and everything you do, including investing in stocks, should start with them. For simplicity's sake, we describe four investment styles. All require commitment and work, and all can be successful. They are really points on a continuum ranging from extremely conservative to quite aggressive. Every investor is different. But by comparing these brief vignettes to your situation and goals, you can begin developing your own investment style.

Building Your Portfolio: The Young Long-term Investor

Many people begin serious investing in the stock market when they reach their forties and fifties. With retirement coming in a few years, they attempt to play catch-up and hope for large returns to fund their retirement nest egg. To this end, more than half the families in the United States are invested in the stock market. Why do they choose to own stocks? Because for the last one hundred years, the returns from the stock market have outpaced other popular kinds of investments like bonds and certificates of deposits.

But the stock market doesn't go up every year. In fact, there have been periods when the stock market went down for several years or was flat for many years. If you are middle-aged and happen to invest during an off period, you may not accumulate enough money in your stock portfolio to fund your retirement. However, if you invest at a very young age and hold your investments for a long time, say forty or fifty years, you can counteract the ups and downs of the market and you will have a very good chance of making lots of money. The secret is to invest for a long time.

Thus, the best plan is to start investing at the earliest possible age. With a rising long-term stock market and many years of investing, you are almost certain to achieve large long-term returns. For example, $1,000 invested each year in the United States stock market from 1954 to 2003, grew to $537,493 as of June 25, 2004. So a $50,000 investment grew tenfold. This simple example shows that you don't have to be wealthy to make money in the market. You simply need a modest amount of money, discipline to invest regularly, and lots of time. Obviously no one knows what the future will bring for the stock market, but if you assume the long-term future will be somewhat like the last fifty years, you should make lots of money investing in stocks.

Just imagine how much money you could accumulate if you start a systematic savings and investment program when you are eighteen and continued the program throughout your adult life. Teens and young adults have money at their disposal. Many receive a regular allowance from their parents. Many have part-time or full-time jobs. Most kids receive money from their parents and relatives on birthdays, special religious celebrations, and holidays. Some are given money for academic and other achievements. Often, high school and college seniors receive money as a graduation present. And cash gifts are common as wedding presents.

In our affluent world, teens and young adults are consumers like all of us. So they tend to spend much of the money they receive and earn. Most young people spend money on clothes, food, and entertainment. Many own cars and others have expensive hobbies. Some are in college or on their own and pay rent and utilities. But although saving money may be difficult, it's very important that young people become regular savers and investors. Because they have lots of time on their side, their investment dollars have the potential of making huge gains.

The following list is your roadmap to profitable investing for a lifetime.

1. Start a systematic savings program at the earliest age.
2. Open a Roth Individual Retirement Account (IRA) at a low-cost financial institution.
3. Begin making contributions to your IRA as soon as you earn taxable income from a part-time or full-time job.
4. Own shares of the five hundred largest companies in the United States by owning the Standard & Poor's 500 stock index (S&P 500).

5. Reinvest all dividends you receive.
6. Set up a systematic schedule of contributions.
7. Hold your shares until you retire.

Each of the seven steps is easy to understand and implement. The following discussion gives you specific recommendations and instructions how to construct your lifetime investing program.

Before you can invest your money for the long term, you must have the money to invest. Many people spend their money so quickly that they don't have any left to save and invest. You want to learn how to avoid the "no savings" trap.

To save money requires that you discipline yourself to set aside some percentage of your income, allowance, and monetary gifts *before* you spend that money. As a start, think about saving at least 10 percent of your income, monetary gifts, and allowance. If you can save a higher percentage, that's even better. Remember that the more you save and invest at the earliest possible age, the more money you'll have in the future.

Follow these five simple rules to save money.

- Save first, then spend, and make **saving**, not spending, your top priority.
- Save money every time you receive money; get into the savings habit, be a disciplined saver.
- Save as much as you can; even a few dollars saved is better than nothing saved.

- As your income increases, save more; save added income, don't spend it all.
- Save forever; continue to save even when you feel you have enough money. Because of inflation (rising cost of living), money doesn't go as far as you might think.

Finally, think about this idea: "Having money doesn't ensure happiness but not having money makes happiness more difficult." One of the best ways to save is to have a percentage of each pay check routed to a savings or money market account automatically. This is easy to set up at your bank or brokerage house, and can be done on line.

We recommend investing in the broad United States stock market as defined by the Standard & Poor's 500 stock index. This index includes the five hundred largest publicly traded companies in the United States. Thus, it is a diverse mix of all types of companies like IBM, General Electric, Microsoft, and Colgate that provide goods and services to the United States and the world. With the S&P 500, you don't have to attempt to pick a few stocks that may or may not do well. You can sleep well knowing that your diversified portfolio of five hundred companies will protect you from a few bad apples. As a shareholder of the S&P 500, you are entitled to benefit from the good fortune of these companies; so as they grow their businesses and profits, their stock prices will increase and you'll make money from this price appreciation. Some of the companies will generate excess cash and distribute it to shareholders in the form of cash dividends. You may take the dividends in cash or reinvest them and buy more shares of stock. We recommend that you reinvest the dividends. The combination of dividends and stock price appreciation ensures that your long-run returns will be greater than most other investments. Of course there will be periods when the stock market is doing well and some years when it's doing poorly. But over the long run, you can expect the S&P 500 to rise in price.

The U.S. stock market includes thousands of stocks and mutual funds. With all these choices available, why do we recommend the S&P 500? The primary reason is because it is very difficult to pick stocks and mutual funds that have a better **long-term** performance (makes you more money) than the S&P 500. Most professionally managed mutual funds do less well than the S&P 500 in the long run. Of course some funds do better, but it takes lots of time and study to pick the winners. The same is true with individual stocks. If you pick a winner, you can make huge amounts of money in a short time. But you can also lose a lot of money very quickly if you pick a loser.

The next step is to establish a retirement account at a financial institution where you can regularly buy the S&P 500 and keep some cash. I recommend that you set up a Roth Individual Retirement (IRA) account. The U.S. government established the Roth IRA to encourage people to save for their long-term financial needs. The primary advantage of the Roth IRA is that you never pay any tax on gains that you achieve in the account. This tax-shelter feature is a boon to investors because taxes take a big chunk of your investment returns. You may set up a Roth IRA at any age when you begin to receive earned income from a part-time or full-time job. Earned income is money you receive in wages, tips, and salaries. Gifts and allowance money do not qualify as earned income. You can contribute $1 for each $1 of earned income up to a maximum of $3,000 for one calendar year. If you have no earned income for a year, you cannot make any contributions to your IRA for that year.

You may start to withdraw money from the Roth IRA after age fifty-nine and a half and you'll pay absolutely no taxes on any gains you made on your investments in the account. If you withdraw money before fifty-nine and a half, you must pay substantial penalties. Remember that the Roth IRA is intended as a retirement buy-and-hold account for long-term investing. So if you need money for immediate purposes like school, travel, and medical expenses, do not put that money in your IRA account. Once the money is in the IRA account it should stay there until you retire.

You can set up a Roth IRA at most banks, brokerage firms, and mutual-fund companies. I recommend that you select a financial institution that:

- offers an S&P 500 option (some institutions do not offer the S&P 500);
- charges very low fees—fees can substantially reduce your returns;
- offers automatic investing; you may want to make automatic investments each month or another time interval.

You can buy the S&P 500 through a special type of mutual fund called an index fund that mirrors the return of the

Standard & Poor's 500 stock index. The index fund is not actively managed so it is very inexpensive to run compared to a managed mutual fund that requires hands-on buying and selling of stock. The lowest fee index fund that tracks the S&P 500 is the Vanguard 500 Index Trust Investor Shares. It owns the five hundred companies that comprise the S&P 500. You can buy the Vanguard 500 Index Fund Investor Shares directly from the Vanguard Group, a leading low-cost mutual fund company.

Another way to own the S&P 500 is with an exchange-traded fund (ETF), which you can buy and sell like a stock. The exchange-traded fund that tracks the S&P 500 is called the SPY. You can purchase shares of the SPY from any brokerage firm. You will pay a small commission to buy the SPY and another small commission to sell it. But unlike a mutual fund, you will not pay any annual fees to own it in your account. Either the Vanguard Index 500 or the SPY is appropriate for your Roth IRA.

All retirement accounts are subject to fees charged by the financial institution. Try to minimize these fees because they add up and will reduce your total return. Even seemingly small fees can have a significant impact on your total returns. The types of fees include a set-up fee to open the account, a transaction fee to buy and sell an investment, an annual fee to maintain the account, an inactivity fee for an account with few or no transactions, a redemption fee for withdrawing money, and a transfer fee to transfer your account from one institution to another. Also, many accounts have a minimum dollar amount required to open an account. Take time to understand fully the fee structure before you open an account.

A company that generates excess cash that it doesn't need for operations often distributes that cash to its shareholders in the form of cash dividends. Many of the five hundred companies that comprise the S&P 500 stock index pay dividends. Therefore, the Vanguard 500 Index Trust Investor Shares and the Spy pass along dividends to their shareholders. For example, on May 26, 2004, the Vanguard 500 Index Trust Investor Shares paid a $0.36 quarterly dividend for each share that an investor owned. If you owned one thousand shares, you would have received $360 in dividends. Because the fund pays a dividend four times each year you would expect to receive approximately $1,400 in dividends for the year. You may receive the dividends in cash or you may reinvest them and buy additional shares. We recommend that you always reinvest the dividends. With them you increase the number of shares you own without contributing any new money to your account.

Discipline and convenience are the keys to regular savings and investing. When you have a steady stream of earned income from a part-time or full-time job, you can decide to regularly invest a fixed amount of money to your Roth IRA. For example, you could contribute $100 each month. The most convenient method to invest regularly is to set up an automatic transfer from your checking or savings account to your Roth IRA account. Most IRA accounts let you set up the transfers online. So in a few minutes you simply specify the dollar amount of the transfer, the day of the month of the transfer, and your bank account information (routing and account numbers). With automatic investing you add new money to your IRA at regular intervals. This means that when you invest new money, you will be buying the S&P 500 at different prices. When the market is down, you'll buy more shares than when the market is up. This process is called dollar-cost averaging because the cost of all your shares is the average of what you paid for each share. Some shares were cheap and some were more expensive. Dollar-cost averaging is a simple way of systematically investing for the long-term.

So what could go wrong with the lifetime plan of investing in the entire stock market using the S&P 500? The worst-case scenario would be for the U.S. economy to crumble for a long period just before or during your retirement. In this case your portfolio would lose value when you needed to withdraw money. If you were concerned that a prolonged downturn was coming, there are investment tactics that you could execute to protect your portfolio from serious losses. The simplest would be to sell some of your stock and keep the proceeds in cash. You probably would not make much interest from the cash but you would not lose a lot of money if stock prices were to fall. But obviously, no one knows what economic conditions will be in fifty years. So at a young age you should be more concerned about saving and investing today rather than worrying about what could happen in fifty years.

Building Your Portfolio: The Conservative Investor

This investor doesn't have the time horizon that someone starting to invest in their early twenties does, but still has relatively distant goals: college for young children or grandchildren, retirement, or the building of an estate to pass on. Also, this investor doesn't want to spend a major amount of time on portfolio management.

Thus the approach described here is for the long-term (ten years or more), cautious buy-and-hold investor who wants a safe portfolio that will grow in value but one that does not require constant attention. The approach is not a get-rich-quick scheme and does not promise to double or triple your money overnight, in a few months, or even in a few years. Rather, with patience and perseverance, you'll build and manage a robust stock portfolio that grows in value year after year and protects you from serious losses. The strategy is based on the well-known sound-investing principles of buy-and-hold, diversification, dollar-cost averaging, and dividend reinvestment (for a more detailed discussion of these concepts, see the next chapter). When you apply these techniques properly for a long period, you will be rewarded with a money-making stock portfolio. And you'll have the satisfaction that comes from building and maintaining it.

The simplest way to participate in the United States stock market is to own a low-cost mutual fund that tracks the S&P 500. Another easy way to get started is to own a few stocks that pay dividends. For more information, read "Starter Portfolio and Dividend Reinvestment Portfolio." Still another conservative approach to investing is to own the Dow Jones Select Dividend Index Fund, an exchange-traded fund that owns fifty large dividend-paying stocks. Read "All about Dividends" for more information on dividends, dividend-paying stocks, and dividend-paying mutual funds.

Because the cautious investor chooses not to be too daring, you should buy broad market index funds, exchange-traded funds, low-fee equity income mutual funds, or a few blue-chip stocks. And keep some cash so you can buy stocks at a bargain price. You can safely buy these investments and not have to watch them day after day. Yes, their prices will move up and down, but over the long run, their prices will rise and you'll make money. Be very wary of most managed mutual funds. Some managed funds have outstanding long-term performance records but most don't do better than the S&P 500, the benchmark against which fund performance is measured. And these funds charge you significantly higher fees. So you may underperform the S&P 500 and still have to pay excessive fees. This is not a good deal.

If you want to spend some time researching stocks, you could build your own mutual fund of well-known companies that pay dividends. For more information about building a mutual fund, read "Building Your Own Mutual Fund."

There are many ways to combine these investments. There is not just one optimal combination. For example, you could own only the S&P 500, or you could own the S&P 500 and a collection of other stocks. Finally, you could own only individual stocks. No matter the mix of investments, always keep 10 percent to 20 percent of your portfolio in cash so you can buy bargains as they come along. You do not have to be "fully invested" (all your money committed to stocks).

You should not buy cyclical stocks or mutual funds that

concentrate on cyclical stocks because of their wide price fluctuations. To make money on cyclical stocks, you have to time your purchases and sales, which would require you to regularly follow price changes. Also, avoid mutual funds that concentrate on a single industry. These specialized funds make money as long as the industry they represent does well, but when the industry turns down, the fund price falls. For example, a mutual fund of only technology stocks tracks the technology cycle and is not truly diversified. Finally, ignore mutual funds that concentrate on foreign countries. Some of these country funds may do well but many are quite volatile. A key to profitable investing is not to pay too much for an investment. Stocks, bonds, real estate, and commodities go up and down in price. It's important that you buy when prices are going up (known as the upside). And of equal importance is not to buy when prices are falling (the downside). When you buy on the upside, you have a good chance that prices will rise after you buy. But if you buy on the downside, chances are good that prices will continue to fall; a stock that dropped from $50 to $10 was not a bargain at $35. Of course, if you bought on the upside near the peak price, you probably won't make money either. So even when you buy on the upside, you have to careful not to pay too much.

Building a money-making retirement portfolio need not be a daunting task. If you follow the guidelines in this book and other articles on *buyupside.com*, you should be able to make thoughtful investment choices that will ensure that you meet your financial goals.

Building Your Portfolio: The Aggressive Investor

The aggressive investor:

- is committed to learning about stocks and the stock market and spends lots of time thinking about stocks and investing;
- takes chances and "bets" on speculative stocks;
- likes the "action" of the market;
- trades stocks in the short term;
- is not afraid to lose money.

If you fit most of these characteristics, you qualify as an aggressive investor.

In addition to any investment owned by the cautious investor, the aggressive investor can own the following:

- speculative stocks—usually small to medium market cap fast-growing companies whose price is volatile;
- cyclical stocks—stocks with a price pattern that has a prolonged upside followed by prolonged downside, making them good stocks to trade;
- blue-chip stocks—well-managed companies with steady growth in revenues and earnings and a stock price with a prolonged upside. These are good stocks to trade for a predetermined profit or to buy-and-hold;
- options—buy a call to bet on an upside price move and put a bet on a downside price move.

The aggressive investor can open a margin account with a brokerage firm and buy on margin and can sell short to bet on a downside price move.

When to Buy
The aggressive investor needs to be ever mindful not to buy on the downside and not to pay too much for a stock. Before you invest, read the rest of this book and "Buy on the Upside and Never Buy on the Downside," "Buying at the Peak," "Bubbles," and "Making Buy Decisions" on the Web site.

When to Sell
Sell when you have a predetermined profit, prices go to the downside, or the company gets into trouble. Don't sell a good company just because its price is down. Hold the stock and wait for the price to recover. If you buy a stock and realize that you made a bad decision (for whatever reason), sell it immediately. Take a small loss or gain and move on. For more information about selling stocks, read "Making Sell Decisions."

To make money consistently, always buy a quality stock at the right price (don't pay too much). Don't buy on the downside and sell when you have a substantial profit, but don't get greedy.

Building Your Portfolio: A Retirement Focus
Planning for a comfortable retirement takes thought and discipline. You can start the process by answering the following questions: How much money will I need for

retirement? What will be my monthly and annual expenses? What will inflation do to my nest egg? How much money should I have when I retire? How much money will I get from Social Security and pensions from former employers? How much money will my own savings and investments have to provide? How can I ensure that I won't run out of money? These questions prompt another set of equally important questions that include the following: When should I start saving for my retirement? How much should I invest each year? What investments should I own?

During your working years you'll need to save and invest for your retirement. Your retirement portfolio will grow in dollar value from the new money you add plus from the interest, dividends, and capital gains you receive from your investments. It takes a huge amount of money to both generate an adequate stream of income year after year and not erode the principal. Therefore, it's very important to start saving and investing for your future retirement needs at the earliest possible age.

Here are the steps that you should follow to plan your retirement portfolio.

1. Estimate your income for the first year of your retirement from Social Security, pensions, and any other assured sources.
2. Estimate your annual retirement expenses for the first year of your retirement.
3. Compute the difference between your total income and expenses. This amount (gap) is what you have to

provide from your savings and investments for the first year of your retirement.
4. Project the gap forward for the number of years you wish to plan for after retirement. This total approximates your retirement needs.
5. Estimate how much money you must accumulate to satisfy your retirement needs. That is your retirement target.
6. Determine how much money you must invest to reach your retirement target.
7. Set up a savings plan.
8. Set up an investing plan.
9. Execute the savings and investment plans and adjust them as you get better information (as you get closer to retirement you can refine your estimates of income and expenses).

Estimate Your Annual Retirement Income

Determine all your noninvestment sources of income that you'll receive during retirement. Check with the Social Security Administration and your current and past employers to determine your projected retirement benefits. Also, include any other sources of retirement income such as help from your family or part-time work. Add all these incomes to get your total outside income.

Estimate Your Annual Retirement Expenses

The next step in your retirement planning is to estimate your annual expenses during retirement. Start by estimating your expenses for the first year of retirement. You'll need to make many assumptions and estimates about future spending, but that's part of the retirement planning process. Your estimates don't have to be accurate down to the penny. Just be sure to include all types of retirement expenses like housing, utilities, car, clothes, food, medical, insurance, taxes, vacations, gifts, and any other expenses. The total expenses for your first year of retirement are the baseline for the next step, which is to determine how much money you must accumulate to meet your retirement expenses.

Compute the Amount of Money You Must Provide

To determine how much *additional* money you'll need to provide from your savings and investments, subtract your total expenses from the total outside income. The difference is the dollar amount you must provide annually. For example, assume your outside income is $20,000 per year and your expenses are $40,000 per year. Then you would have to provide another $20,000 each year from your savings and investments.

How Much Money Must You Accumulate?

After you have determined how much money you need to provide from your savings and investments for your first year of retirement, you can determine how much money you'll need to accumulate. Do the following:

1. Decide how many years you'll need money after you retirement.
2. Select the average inflation rate for the retirement period.
3. Select the average rate of return on your investments for the retirement period.

Given this information, you can estimate how much money you'll need to accumulate before you retire so you'll have enough money to meet your retirement financial needs.

How Many Years You'll Need Money after Your Retirement

Answering this question is difficult because you're asking how long you (and perhaps your spouse) expect to live. And no one wants to answer that question. So pick a number, say thirty to forty years, that is the outside limit of your retirement years assuming you retire at sixty-five (or another age). Remember that if you were born in 1939 or later, your Social Security doesn't start at your sixty-fifth birthday but later, depending on your year of birth. Don't pick too low a number of years because if you live long enough, you'll run out of money and be old *and* poor.

Select the Average Inflation Rate

Inflation increases your expenses each year. Some years inflation is high, and other years it's low. From 2000 to 2003, the annual inflation rate was around 2 percent, which is relatively low by historical measures. No one knows what the rate of inflation will be in the next thirty years. But you have to make an estimate because we know it will cause your retirement expenses to increase. A reasonable estimate is somewhere between 4 to 7 percent.

Select the Average Investment Rate of Return

No one knows for sure what stocks and interest rates will do in the future. But we do have historical data to help us make reasonable guesses. For example, stocks have returned at least 5 percent to 6 percent annual returns over long periods.

Currently, interest rates are at historical lows but probably will increase. So you can use a conservative estimate for stocks of 6 percent, and interest rates of 5 percent. When you select your estimates, don't be too optimistic about your returns. The prospect of future high returns could lead you to save and invest too little money.

How Much to Accumulate: An Example

Let's assume you need to withdraw $20,000 from your retirement account the first year of retirement. Remember the $20,000 is in addition to Social Security and pension income. After that each year, you'll withdraw $20,000 adjusted for inflation. This means that as inflation increases you'll withdraw more than $20,000 each year. Inflation is included in the analysis because in real time, inflation erodes the buying power of the dollar, so that $20,000 twenty years from now won't buy you the same basket of goods that $20,000 will buy today. Therefore, each year you must increase the amount you withdraw to keep up with inflation. For example, an inflation rate of 6 percent would cause you to withdraw $60,511.99 in year twenty, and $108,367.76 in year thirty. The effect of inflation can't be taken lightly. It is the "silent killer" of your long-term financial well-being.

The next table shows for different rates of return and inflation the *required starting balance* of a retirement account given you intend to withdraw money for *thirty years* with a $20,000 withdrawal the first year, and a $20,000 annual withdrawal adjusted for inflation for years two through thirty. At the end of thirty years, the balance of the account will be near or at zero dollars. The selected rate of return and inflation rate are assumed to stay constant for each year of the thirty-year period.

Table 1. Retirement account balances at the beginning of retirement required to allow an annual withdrawal of $20,000 adjusted for inflation for thirty years under different inflation and rate of return assumptions.

Starting Balance of Retirement Account
Year 1 Withdrawal Is $20,000,
Years 2–30 Withdrawals Are Adjusted for Inflation
Withdrawal Period Is 30 Years

	Rate of Return During Withdrawal Period					
Inflation	0%	2%	4%	6%	8%	10%
0%	$600,000	$448,000	$346,000	$276,000	$226,000	$189,000
2%	$811,000	$589,000	$423,000	$343,000	$274,000	$206,000
4%	$1,122,000	$791,000	$577,000	$436,000	$339,000	$254,000
6%	$1,590,000	$1,090,000	$781,000	$567,000	$430,000	$318,000
8%	$2,270,000	$1,520,000	$1,060,000	$753,000	$556,000	$424,000
10%	$3,290,000	$2,160,000	$1,460,000	$1,020,000	$735,000	$746,000

The worst-case scenario is a starting balance of $3,290,000 for a 0 percent return and 10 percent inflation during the withdrawal period. The best-case scenario is a starting balance of $189,000 for no inflation and a 10 percent return. Both of these scenarios are unlikely. The first one says "keep your money in your mattress" and the second assumes "an almost perfect world." A more likely scenario is moderate inflation and a modest rate of return. For example, a 4 percent inflation rate and a 6 percent annual rate of return for which you need a starting balance of $436,000 to maintain the required thirty-year stream of income.

What do these figures tell us and how can we use them to effectively save for retirement? First, it takes a lot of money to generate a long-term stream of income, particularly at low rates of return combined with high inflation. Second, investors who can maintain high rates of returns can start with less money compared to those investors who earn smaller rates of return. Third, you can't control inflation; you can only hedge against it. And the ways you do that are to get high returns and start with the largest pile of money you can. The large pile acts as a cushion against both inflation and fluctuating rates of return.

Investment Schedules: How Much You Must Invest

Now you need to determine how much you need to invest to achieve the target balance for your first year of retirement. The two key questions that require answers are: How much money must I invest each month? How many years must I make these investments? The next three tables show investment schedules for thirty-, twenty-, and ten-year accumulation periods. Use these tables to determine how much money you need to invest each month for a given number of years to achieve the target amount of money for your first year of retirement. Each table has five alternative rates of return for the accumulation period. The tables show the following relationships between the amount you must invest each year, and the length of the accumulation period, rate or return, and the target amount.

- The higher the target dollar amount, the more you must invest.
- The lower the rate of return, the more you must invest.
- The shorter the period of accumulation, the more you must invest.

Assuming that your investment dollars are limited because of budgetary constraints, you want to make the best use of them. Therefore, it pays to learn about investing so you can increase your returns. Become a committed investor and reap the benefits of knowing how to invest for profitable returns. Also, start investing at the earliest possible age. Although the investment dollars may be difficult to come by when you are young, you don't have to commit as many of them, compared to waiting later when you are nearer to retirement. Let time and compound interest work for you. Here is an example of determining how much you need to invest each month. Assume that you:

- want to have $500,000 in your investment retirement fund by the first year of retirement;
- will receive a 6 percent average rate of return during the accumulation period;
- have a thirty-year accumulation period.

In the following Monthly Investment Schedule (Thirty-year Accumulation Period) find the column labeled 6 percent and the row labeled $500,000. The cell for 6 percent and $500,000 shows that you must invest $498 each month for thirty years, a total of $179,191. If you have only ten years to accumulate $500,000 at 6 percent, the Monthly Investment Schedule (Ten-year Accumulation Period) shows that you must invest $3,051 each month, or a total of $366,123. So if you put off investing, you must make very large monthly investments to reach a target amount of money for your retirement. To make savings and investing affordable, you must start investing at the earliest possible age.

Table 2. Monthly investment needed over a thirty-year accumulation period to accumulate a range of balances at the beginning of retirement.

Monthly Investment Schedule
30-year Accumulation Period
Rate of Return

Initial Balance	2%	4%	6%	8%	10%
$50,000	$101	$72	$50	$34	$22
$100,000	$203	$144	$100	$67	$44
$200,000	$406	$288	$199	$134	$88
$300,000	$609	$432	$299	$201	$133
$400,000	$812	$576	$398	$268	$177
$500,000	$1,015	$720	$498	$335	$221
$1,000,000	$2,030	$1,441	$996	$671	$442
$2,000,000	$4,059	$2,882	$1,991	$1,342	$885

The following table contains the required monthly investments for a twenty-year accumulation period.

Table 3. Monthly investment needed over a twenty-year accumulation period to accumulate a range of balances at the beginning of retirement.

Monthly Investment Schedule
20-year Accumulation Period
Rate of Return

Initial Balance	2%	4%	6%	8%	10%
$50,000	$170	$136	$108	$85	$66
$100,000	$339	$273	$216	$170	$132
$200,000	$678	$545	$433	$340	$263
$300,000	$1,018	$818	4649	$509	$395
$400,000	$1,357	$1,091	$866	$679	$527
$500,000	$1,696	$1,363	$1,082	$849	$658
$1,000,000	$3,392	$2,726	$2,164	$1,698	$1,317
$2,000,000	$6,784	$5,453	$4,329	$3,395	$2,634

The following table contains the required monthly investments for a ten-year accumulation period.

Table 4. Monthly investment needed over a ten-year accumulation period to accumulate a range of balances at the beginning of retirement.

Monthly Investment Schedule
10-year Accumulation Period
Rate of Return

Initial Balance	2%	4%	6%	8%	10%
$50,000	$377	$340	$305	$273	$244
$100,000	$753	$679	$610	$547	$488
$200,000	$1,507	$1,358	$1,220	$1,093	$976
$300,000	$2,260	$2,037	$1,831	$1,640	$1,465
$400,000	$3,014	$2,716	$2,441	$2,186	$1,953
$500,000	$3,767	$3,396	$3,051	$2,733	$2,441
$1,000,000	$7,535	$6,791	$6,102	$5,466	$4,882
$2,000,000	$15,069	$13,582	$12,204	$10,932	$9,763

The following table summarizes the required monthly investments for a 6 percent rate of return for the three different investment periods.

Table 5. Monthly investment needed at a 6 percent rate of return to achieve initial retirement balances over ten-, twenty-, and thirty-year accumulation periods.

Monthly Investment Schedule Summary
Rate of Return Is 6%
Accumulation Period

Initial Balance	10	20	30
$50,000	$305	$108	$50
$100,000	$610	$216	$100
$200,000	$1,220	$433	$199
$300,000	$1,831	$649	$299
$400,000	$2,441	$866	$398
$500,000	$3,051	$1,082	$498
$1,000,000	$6,102	$2,164	$996
$2,000,000	$12,204	$4,329	$1,991

Future Value of a Monthly Investment

Many people set aside a fixed dollar amount each month that they can afford to save and invest. With this approach the amount you invest is dictated by how much you decide to save each month not by how much money you want to accumulate. There is nothing wrong with this approach as long as you know what you'll end up accumulating. If that amount is not enough to start your retirement, then you can decide how much more money you'll need to invest each month or whether to retire later.

The following table shows how much money you'll accumulate for different monthly amounts invested at 6 percent rate of return for ten-, twenty-, and thirty-year accumulation periods.

Table 6. Outcomes of a range of monthly investments for a 6 percent rate of return over ten-, twenty-, and thirty-year accumulation periods.

Future Value of Monthly Investments
Rate of Return Is 6%
Accumulation Period

Monthly Investment	10	20	30
$50	$8,235	$23,218	$50,477
$100	$16,470	$46,435	$100,954
$200	$32,940	$92,870	$201,908
$300	$49,410	$139,305	$302,861
$400	$65,879	$185,740	$403,815
$500	$82,349	$232,176	$504,769
$1,000	$164,699	$464,351	$1,009,538
$2,000	$329,397	$928,702	$2,019,075

As the other investment schedules show, you accumulate lots of money if you start investing early in your life. For example, you accumulate over $300,000 with a $300 per month investment for thirty years. But the same $300 invested monthly for ten years gives you only $49,100.

Setting Up a Savings Plan

You have to save money first before you can invest it. How much money you spend and save is strictly up to you. But remember, the more you save and invest at a young age, the less money you have to invest later. We offer no specific advice other than set up a budget, control buying on credit, make saving money a very important priority, and save some money each pay period. Any amount saved is better than no amount saved. Get into the habit of saving money. The more money that you save and invest at a young age, the more money you'll have in your pocket in older age.

CHAPTER 4

Alice in Wonderland

Alice confronted the strange world she found on the other side of the looking glass with amazing equanimity. It is imperative that you as an investor confront the reality you see, not how you think things ought to be or how others tell you they are.

For example, not all owners of Wal-Mart (WMT) stock are rich even though the stock increased over nine hundredfold from 1972 to 2002. Table 1 shows the very different outcomes for five WMT investors after they each invested $1,000.

Investor number 1 bought 15515.18 shares in 1972, held the shares and their market value on April 12, 2002, was $949,995. This is a buy-and-hold success story! Investor number 2 bought the same number of shares as investor number 1, but sold them after a tenfold increase in less than ten years. Investor number 3 bought shares in 1992, held them through a flat price pattern, and sold in 1997 with a tiny gain. Investor number 4 successfully timed the purchase and sale to get a sixfold return in less than two years. The last investor bought near the 1999 peak price and as of April 20, 2002, was losing money. The message here is that "buy and hold" is successful, depending on when you buy and how long you hold. The committed investor makes careful decisions based on detailed knowledge about both when to buy and how long to hold.

Table 7. Effect of buy-and-sell dates on investor outcomes for Wal-Mart stock.

	Buy Date	Buy Price	# Shares	Sell Date	Sell Price	Sell Value
Investor #1	8/25/1972	$0.06	15515.18	4/12/2002	$61.23	$949,995
Investor #2	8/25/1972	$0.06	15515.18	11/3/1982	$0.67	$10,364
Investor #3	3/1/1992	$13.31	75.12	3/3/1997	$13.5	$1,014
Investor #4	1/27/1997	$11.44	87.43	12/27/1999	$69.44	$6,071
Investor #5	12/27/1999	$69.44	14.4	4/12/2002	$61.23	$882

Similarly, the committed investor tracks each stock in her portfolio and avoids becoming wedded to any single stock. Three stocks, AOL, BS, and CL, present vastly different patterns over a time when the general market peaked and then declined. Obviously, for the period chosen, an investor in each of the stocks fared wildly differently. Just as obviously, riding BS down through a period of market increase did not produce the kind of "historic return" often touted for equities. Thus, being married to any stock on general principle is a bad thing.

Figure 2. Price chart of three contrasting stock price patterns over time.

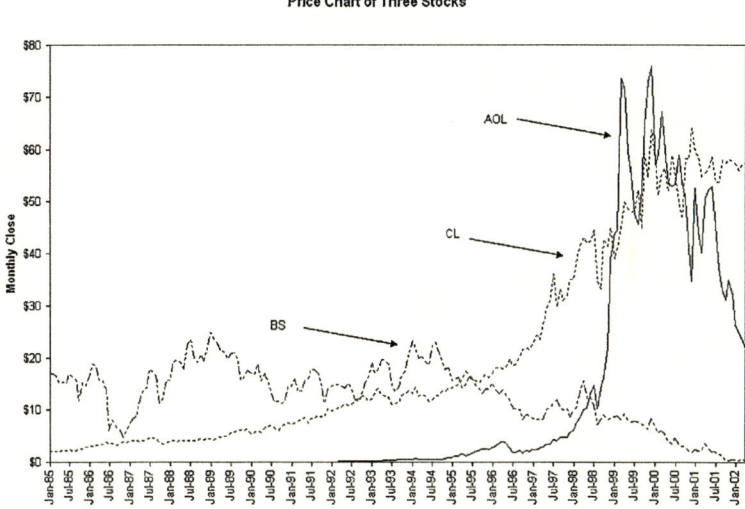

Neither is holding a "market index" portfolio a foolproof and mindless way for the noncommitted investor to thrive. Figure 3 shows the Standard and Poor 500 index from 1900 projected to 2020. The patterns of the past, although not by any means a foolproof guide to the future, strongly indicate that the S&P index will be "range-bound" for a relatively long time, perhaps ten years or more. If that is so, the committed investor will have to carefully pick and trade stocks to make money.

Figure 3. The S&P 500 index for 1900-2001, adjusted for inflation with trading range indicated.

Buy and Hold

We nevertheless advocate that you should buy and hold stocks for the long run. Your alternative is to repeatedly buy stocks at low prices and sell them at higher prices. If this were easy to do, we would encourage you to do it. But prices move up and down in patterns that are difficult to understand unless you judiciously study charts and perform detailed technical analysis of price patterns. And even then, it's difficult to consistently "time" your transactions so that you would make money. We recommend that you buy well-managed dividend-paying companies, index funds, or low-fee managed mutual funds and hold them for a long time. If you have ten or more years, you can wait out declines in price and hopefully sell your stocks for a profit when you need the money.

BUY ON THE UPSIDE

We illustrate this with two buy-and-hold success stories. The stock market peaked in 1929 before it crashed and sank over 90 percent. This investor waited out the 1929 euphoria and subsequent crash and bought in 1932 after the market had found a bottom. The following chart shows how the investor's $1,000 investment grew.

Figure 4. The DJIA portfolio value with initial investment in 1932 by an investor aged fifty years.

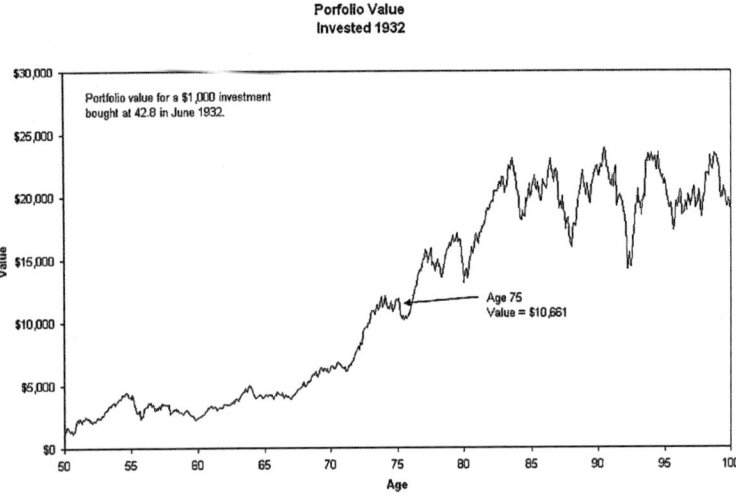

When the investor was seventy-five, the portfolio was worth over $10,000,000 and growing. Yes, there were significant fluctuations in value as the DJIA prices moved up and down, but this investor experienced real wealth creation.

I know of a friend of a friend who is one hundred years old. The value of her portfolio of blue-chip stocks is in the low seven figures. Suppose she had invested $1,000 at age fifty in 1953. The next chart shows the spectacular results of buy-and-hold investing.

Figure 5. The DJIA portfolio value with initial investment in 1953 by an investor aged fifty years.

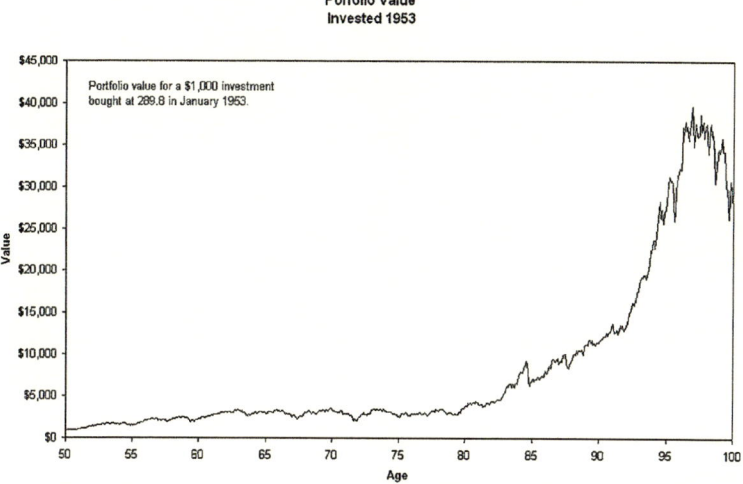

At the market peak in 2000, the $1,000 had grown to over $40,000. Even with the price decline since the peak, she still has over $25,000.

The previous two examples showed the benefits of buy-and-hold investing. When you buy at a reasonable price and prices are in a long-term up trend, you can make a lot of money. But what happens to your returns if prices move down for a long time after you buy? The Japanese stock market provides data for such a case. Assume you wanted to diversify your stock holdings to include foreign stocks, so in 1993 you invested in the Nikkei 225, the Japanese market equivalent of the DJIA. You knew the N225 had peaked in 1989 at 38,916 and you thought the subsequent decline in price to 17,024 gave you a great buying opportunity. So at age fifty you invested $1,000. The next chart shows the ensuing disaster.

Figure 6. The Nikkei 225 portfolio value with initial investment in 1993 by an investor aged fifty years.

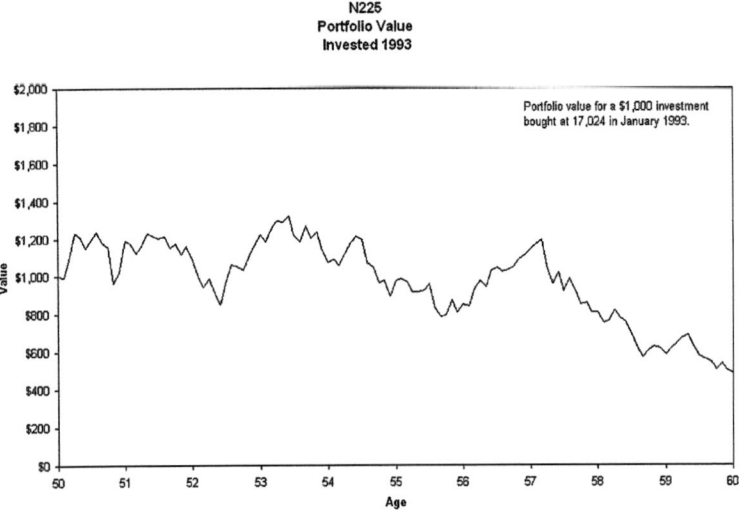

As of the February 2003 close at 8513.54, the investment was worth $500. Buy-and-hold investing for this downside price pattern was a mistake. Even dollar-cost averaging would not have averted a disaster because prices kept falling. No one knows what stock prices will do in the future. I assume that the U.S. economy and the U.S. stock market will trend to the upside for the long run. If this assumption is correct, a long-term buy-and-hold strategy will make you money. If not, you'll lose money.

Dividend Reinvestment

Dividend reinvestment is a systematic method of accumulating shares of a stock that pays a dividend. Most investors use dividend reinvestment as part of a long-term buy-and-hold investment program. After you purchase a stock, simply enroll in the dividend reinvestment plan (DRIP) and your dividends will be automatically used to purchase additional shares. Also, you may send voluntary contributions to purchase additional shares.

During the time you hold the stock and reinvest dividends, you are practicing dollar-cost averaging. At higher stock prices, the dividends buy fewer shares, but at lower prices they buy more shares. You win in the long run as long as the current stock price is greater than your average cost per share. For example, if you own one hundred shares at an average cost of $10 per share and the current stock price is $20, you're up $10 per share or $1,000. But if your average cost is $10 and the current stock price is $5, you're down $5 per share or $500.

Because dividend reinvestment increases the number of shares you own, in a rising market the market value of your holdings will be greater than if you didn't reinvest dividends. However, if the stock price declines for a long period, the value of your investment will decline, and you can still lose money. Reinvesting dividends can help to reduce losses, but it may not eliminate them. Because you pay taxes on dividends, consider putting dividend reinvestment stocks in a retirement account so you can shelter the dividends from your current tax liability.

Examples of Dividend Reinvesting

This discussion includes five examples of dividend reinvestment for stocks owned by Richard Howard. Therefore, we will describe the examples in his words. All the data are actual numbers taken from dividend reinvestment account statements. The DRIP summary table illustrates the results of dividend reinvesting for one mutual fund and four stocks.

Table 8. Actual examples of the performance of stocks with and without dividend reinvestment from Howard's portfolio.

DRIP Summary
02/25/03

	# Shares With DRIP	# Shares W/O DRIP	Current Price	$ Value With DRIP	$ Value W/O DRIP	Difference	% Increase Due to DRIP
VFINX	85.547	58.979	$77.54	$6,633.31	$4,573.23	$2,060.08	45%
AXP	40.768	39.465	$33.16	$1,351.87	$1,308.67	$43.20	3%
DPL	174.862	93.822	$12.03	$2,103.59	$1,128.68	$974.91	86%
DRE	109.601	81.085	$25.74	$2,821.13	$2,087.13	$734.00	35%
WWY	189.297	158.024	$54.32	$10,282.61	$8,583.84	$1,698.77	2%

As you study these examples, note how relatively modest investments produced handsome returns.

Vanguard 500 Index Fund

I opened an Individual Retirement Account (IRA) in 1987 with the Vanguard Group and bought the Vanguard 500 Index Fund (VFINX), which is a low-fee index fund that tracks the S&P 500. The fund pays distributions in the form of dividends and capital gains. In 1987 I invested $1,513 in eight purchases and bought 58.979 shares. From 1987 through 2002 the fund paid distributions (dividends and capital gains) worth $1,596, which added 26.569 shares to the account. So the total distributions have exceeded what I paid for the original shares.

On February 25, 2003, the account market value was $6,633. Without the reinvested distributions the account would have been worth $4,573. Reinvestment of the distributions increased the number of shares by 45 percent and thus the account value by 45 percent.

American Express

American Express (AXP) is a financial services company best known for its American Express charge card. Its current dividend yield is only 0.97 percent. I included AXP here to illustrate the negligible effect that a low dividend yield has on share accumulation. I bought 39.465 shares AXP in 1997 and the account total was 40.768 shares at the end of 2002, only a 3 percent increase in five years. You don't accumulate shares very rapidly with low-yielding stocks.

Duke Realty

Duke Realty (DRE) is a real estate investment trust (REIT) that specializes in owning and managing industrial and office properties. By law, an REIT must pay out most of its earnings in dividends, so an REIT is a logical choice for a dividend reinvestment plan. From 1996 to 1999, I bought 81.085 shares by investing $1,625. I made many purchases using $25 monthly automatic transfers from my checking account. By December 2002 the plan had paid $558 in dividends and the share total was 109.601, a 35 percent increase in the number of shares. DRE's high yield, currently 7.18 percent, ensured rapid accumulation of shares.

DPL

DPL Inc. (DPL) owns Dayton Power and Light Company, an electric utility serving Ohio. DPL has a long history of paying dividends and its current dividend yield is 7.87 percent. After investing $1,000 from 1989 to 1996 to buy 93.822 shares, reinvesting dividends and receiving three three-for-two stock splits, I have 174.862 shares as of December 2002. Adjusting for the splits, the reinvested dividends have increased the share total by 86 percent. The hefty dividend payout has significantly increased my position in DPL.

Wrigley

Wrigley (WWY), the well-known maker of chewing gum, has a steady history of growing earnings and paying dividends. The current yield is 1.63 percent. Wrigley is one of my favorite companies and I invested $2,600 from 1991 to 1996 to purchase 158.234 shares. Currently my account has 189.297 shares, a 20 percent increase due to dividend reinvestment. And the $2,600 investment has grown to over $10,000, primarily due to price appreciation, but helped by dividend reinvestment.

The saying "it takes money to make money" applies to dividend reinvestment. The more money you have in a dividend reinvestment account, the more shares you'll accumulate over time. And if the stock prices increase as well, you get the additional benefit of owning more shares each at a higher value per share, thereby increasing the total dollar value of the investment.

The share accumulation table shows that you accumulate more shares the longer you reinvest your dividends. Also, higher dividends result in more shares. Obviously, the combination of high yield and lots of time results in some very impressive gains.

The table values assume you start with one share of any stock. Each column heading shows a separate dividend yield. The body of each column shows the number of shares you will have after reinvesting the dividends for the specified number of years.

Table 9. Share accumulation for a range of dividend yields for periods of one to fifty years.

Share Accumulation

Dividend Yield

Years Held	1%	2%	3%	4%	5%	6%	7%	8%
1	1.01	1.02	1.03	1.04	1.05	1.06	1.07	1.08
2	1.02	1.04	1.06	1.08	1.1	1.12	1.14	1.17
3	1.03	1.06	1.09	1.12	1.16	1.19	1.23	1.26
4	1.04	1.08	1.13	1.17	1.22	1.26	1.31	1.36
5	1.05	1.1	1.16	1.22	1.28	1.34	1.4	1.47
6	1.06	1.13	1.19	1.27	1.34	1.42	1.5	1.59
7	1.07	1.15	1.23	1.32	1.41	1.5	1.61	1.71
8	1.08	1.17	1.27	1.37	1.48	1.59	1.72	1.85
9	1.09	1.2	1.3	1.42	1.55	1.69	1.84	2
10	1.1	1.22	1.34	1.48	1.63	1.79	1.97	2.16
20	1.22	1.49	1.81	2.19	2.65	3.21	3.87	4.66
30	1.35	1.81	2.43	3.24	4.32	5.74	7.61	10.06
40	1.49	2.21	3.26	4.8	7.04	10.29	14.97	21.72
50	1.64	2.69	4.38	7.11	11.47	18.42	29.46	46.9

For example, assume the dividend yield is 4 percent. For each share you own, in five years you will own 1.22 shares. In thirty years, you'll own 3.24 shares. If you keep the stock for fifty years, you'll accumulate 7.11 shares for each original share. That's over seven times as many shares for doing nothing but filling out a dividend reinvestment form. If the dividend yield is 5 percent, after fifty years you'll have increased your shares over elevenfold.

Setting Up Your Dividend Reinvestment Account

It's easy to reinvest dividends, but always inquire about the fees associated with reinvesting dividends because some plans charge hefty fees. Remember that any fee, no matter the amount, reduces your profits.

Here are a few ways to set up a dividend reinvestment account, include:

- using a full-service broker—ask your broker for details;
- buying direct from a company—contact a company through its Web site;
- buying from a subscription service—see the *Moneypaper*;[14]
- buying through a bank transfer agent—for example, contact Bank of New York.

Using an internet discount broker who offers DRIPs (both this and the full-service broker offer the advantage of having all your stocks in one place, which ensures easy record keeping and tax and estate planning).

Dividend reinvestment is a conservative method for the patient investor who wants to accumulate shares of a stock for the long term. To help you make money, follow these recommendations:

- buy stocks with a stable or increasing dividend;
- check the dividend pay out ratio, dividends/earnings—check if a high ratio (greater than 80 percent) can be sustained;
- consider selling the stock if the company decreases or terminates its dividends or radically changes it business focus;
- monitor the stock's price pattern—buy shares with new money when the stock price falls temporarily if the stock is on the upside;
- consider selling the stock if it makes a bubble top.

Systematic accumulation of shares through dividend reinvestment of a well-managed financially sound company can help increase the value of your portfolio.

For more information about dividend reinvestment read "All about Dividends, Dow Jones Select Dividend Index Fund," "Dividend Reinvestment Portfolio," and "Mergent's Dividend Achievers" on buyupside.com.

Dollar-cost Averaging

Dollar-cost averaging is a systematic investing technique used to accumulate shares of stock or a mutual fund over many months or years. You invest a specified amount of money to buy shares at a regular interval, say each month, and then you hold them for the long term.

As the stock price moves up, a specified dollar amount purchases fewer shares, but when the stock price moves down, you buy more shares. The average price per share is computed by dividing the total cost of all shares by the number of shares. Thus, you dollar-cost average.

Typically, buy-and-hold investors use dollar-cost averaging in retirement accounts and dividend reinvestment plans, and fund the purchases with payroll deductions or automatic debits from a bank account. All large mutual funds and many brokerage accounts allow automatic investing. Here is a simple example of dollar-cost averaging. Suppose you invest $100 each month to buy shares of a stock. The following table shows five monthly purchases at different prices and the resulting number of shares and their value.

Table 10. Effects of dollar-cost averaging, investing a fixed amount monthly resulting in purchasing more stock when the price is lower.

Dollar-cost Averaging

Date	Price per Share	$ Invested	# Shares Bought	Total # Shares Owned	Total $ Value
Mar	$50	$100	2	2	$100.00
Apr	$52	$100	1.923	3.923	$204.00
May	$58	$100	1.724	5.647	$327.54
Jun	$56	$100	1.786	7.433	$416.24
Jul	$61	$100	1.639	9.072	$553.41

After five purchases the total amount invested is $500 and you own 9.072 shares. Therefore, the average cost per share is $55.11 ($500/9.072). As of July, the 9.072 shares were worth $553.41.

Dollar-cost Averaging for Pfizer

Pfizer (PFE) investors, who started dollar-cost averaging purchases at $100 per month in 1982, realized a peak value of $423,813 in July 2000. In February 2002 the value was $253,285 for an investment of $25,400. This 997 percent return resulted from a systematic long-term investment plan that coincided with an increasing stock price from 1982 to 2000 and then a price slide. Clearly, dollar-cost averaging made enormous sums of money for these Pfizer shareholders.

Be careful with dollar-cost averaging. It works when prices are on the upside. But if you make repeated purchases on the downside and prices keep falling, you will lose money. Be particularly cautious with individual stocks of poorly managed companies or stocks whose prices have increased rapidly. These stocks can quickly decline from very high prices to very low prices. For cyclical stocks, take profits when prices are high, and begin the process again when they are low.

Diversification

Much is said in the popular investing media about the benefits of diversifying a stock portfolio. Fund managers routinely extol the virtues of diversification to protect the investor's portfolio from volatility and paper and realized losses. Modern portfolio theory urges investors to diversify according to their level of risk. On the other hand, Warren Buffett[15] tells investors to concentrate on stocks they know well. His "focus investing" approach leads investors to place bets on a few stocks with the expectation and hope of picking big winners. We urge the committed investor to achieve a blend of focus and diversity, and not accept either pure mode as appropriate to your situation and goals.

Pros and Cons of a Broadly Diversified Portfolio

A broadly diversified portfolio has enough stocks in it so that its performance is highly correlated with the broad market or a selected sector index. For example, a very broadly diversified portfolio is one with all or most of the S&P 500 stocks. A broadly diversified sector portfolio is one that includes, for example, all the semiconductor stocks in the Philadelphia Semiconductor Index (SOX). The advantages of a very broadly diversified portfolio are:

- one or a few poorly performing stocks do not significantly reduce the overall portfolio performance;
- it requires less active management, with fewer buy-

and-sell decisions, and attendant lower costs;
- performance is highly correlated with broad market or sector indices, and thus does well in a general up market;
- performance will be no worse than the broad market or index.

The disadvantages of a broadly diversified portfolio are:

- an excellently performing stock does not significantly improve the performance of the portfolio, and thus large potential gains are missed;
- performance is highly correlated with the broad market or sector, and thus does poorly in a down market;
- performance usually will not be better than the broad market or index.

Pros and Cons of a Focused Portfolio

A focused portfolio includes fewer stocks than a broadly diversified portfolio. Usually the focused portfolio includes twenty or fewer stocks. Of course, the number of stocks upon which you can focus is limited by your time and other resources. If you can focus on twenty or more stocks, you can have some of the benefits of diversity and focus combined. The advantages of a focused portfolio are:

- an excellently performing stock significantly improves the performance of the portfolio;
- it may not be highly correlated with broad market or sector and therefore may do well in a down market;

- performance may be considerably better than broad market or index.

The disadvantages of a focused portfolio are:

- a poorly performing stock significantly reduces the performance of the portfolio;
- it requires active management and may require frequent buy-and-sell decisions and costs;
- it may not be highly correlated with broad market or sector—it may not do well in an up market;
- its performance may be worse than broad market or index.

Common sense suggests that if you consistently pick winning stocks, you don't need to own many stocks to achieve high returns. In fact, diversification can reduce your returns if you combine lower-performing stocks with your winners. However, if you have difficulty picking winners, you should add more stocks to your portfolio with the expectation that some of the additional stocks will improve the performance of your portfolio.

Picking winners is not easy. It takes experience, time, money, information, and a bit of luck. But the payoff from winners can be very large. If you consistently pick winners, there is little need to diversify. However, if you don't have the time or inclination to study and understand stocks, choose a broadly diversified portfolio. The committed investor will try to do better than that by using a blend of diversity and focus that fits both his or her skill level and financial objectives.

Managed Mutual Funds

Earlier, we explained the virtues of index mutual funds. Managed mutual funds, those that are actively tailored to meet certain investment goals, are popular with many investors and have the virtue of providing professional management and wide diversification. However, we are critical of managed mutual funds, although many, including us, have and do invest in them. Here is why.

Poor Performance

Managed mutual funds pay managers and consultants to pick stocks and decide when to buy and sell them. Some managers do an outstanding job and their funds outperform the market or target industry sector. But most managed funds underperform their index fund counterparts. Much of the underperformance is due to higher fees and some is due to poor stock selection.

High Fees

All mutual funds charge fees to manage your money and high fees substantially reduce your total returns. Annual fees of one and two percent may seem small but such fees are deceptively large when you compute their arithmetic impact on long-term returns. For more information about how fees reduce your long-term returns read "Mutual Fund Fees."

Too Many Funds

There are thousands of managed funds and many hold the same stocks. For example, check a sample of growth funds. You'll see that many of them hold virtually the same stocks and simply package them with different fund names. Why do retail investors need dozens of funds that are essentially the same? Rather than sorting through a tangle of managed mutual funds, you may be better off spending your time researching individual stocks that might give large gains.

Turnover and Taxes

Funds that buy and sell stocks regularly leave the investor with capital gains tax liabilities. Or if prices start to fall and a fund must sell shares to raise money to meet fund redemptions, you can get stuck with an unexpected capital gains tax bill. So you pay taxes and your investment is worth less.

Disappearing Funds

Another mutual fund industry ploy is to dissolve a poorly performing or unpopular fund and merge it with other fund. Therefore, you have to decide if you want to own the new fund, which may not resemble the original fund.

Try to avoid managed mutual funds. Only a few beat their index fund counterparts. Most managed funds charge high fees for lackluster performance.

CHAPTER 5

Brer Rabbit

Brer Rabbit contrived to be thrown into the briar patch as a punishment. But he liked the briar patch and thus took advantage of what his competitors saw as adversity. To a committed investor, certain kinds of apparent adversity can function for you like the briar patch did for Brer Rabbit. You can make an advantage of knowing what to do when a stock or a market turns down. For example, don't sell at market bottoms. But they are notoriously hard to identify. Also, it is unlikely that you will sell at a stock's highest price in any market or cycle. Cole Porter wrote the song "You're the Top" about a lover, and you may find it there, but not likely in the market. So, what can you do?

Technical analysis—the study of the patterns that stock prices and related quantities make over time—can assist you in knowing whether the market or an individual stock is going up or down. Technically based predictions are far from infallible, but are, on the whole, useful as part of your decision support system. Fundamental analysis—the study of the specifics of individual stocks, industries, and markets—is often described as an alternative, and a more realistic one than technical analysis (Louis Ruykesyer insists on describing technical analysts as "elves").

We prefer to use both, and a biological analogy might help. The growth of an organism over time, say the weight of an elephant from birth to death, tends to change in generally predictable ways. If you know the age and the general kind of animal, you can predict something about its weight growth rate (high when young, slow to none in maturity, and perhaps negative near the end). Similarly, cyclical stocks tend to follow generally predictable patterns of price over time. But if you are trying to predict the growth rate of a specific elephant or herd, you will be greatly aided by knowing some specifics, for example, how much it or they have to eat. And it follows that a cyclical stock at the bottom of a cycle won't recover and rise in price again (at least, not very soon) if the company has poor management or unsustainable debt. So the technical/fundamental dichotomy is a false one in the sense that any rational investor will include both in her decision support system, but will rely on neither in isolation to make buy-and-sell decisions.

One of the most important messages of this book to investors is to only buy when prices are on the upside and not to buy when prices are on the downside. The Complete Trading Model (CTM) and the Price Direction Indicator (PDI) are technical analysis tools that explain why these two rules are valid and suggest when to buy or sell. CTM computes the number and frequency of winning and losing trades for any price series. PDI indicates when prices move from the downside to the upside, and vice versa. Thus, based on the price moves, and the relevant fundamental information on company soundness, you can decide whether to buy, sell, or hold. If you document your reasons thus derived for buying and selling, you will at least know when you have made mistakes and how, an indispensable part of the learning process. CTM and PDI analysis of the price series of all types of stocks and other investments shows conclusively that buying on the upside leads to profits most of the time and buying on the downside leads to losses most of the time. For definition of CTM and PDI terms and concepts see www.buyupside.com.

Interpreting Stock Price Patterns

To successfully implement the "buy on the upside" and "don't buy on the downside" recommendations, you must obviously know whether current prices are on the upside or the downside. This article discusses the most frequently occurring price patterns so you can recognize them as you monitor a real-time price series. Knowing what to look for as prices change helps you make better-informed buy-and-sell decisions. Stock prices move up and down over time and these price movements have recognizable patterns. A price pattern describes how a stock, sector, or market index changes over time. The four basic price patterns are:

- rising prices;
- declining prices;
- sideways prices;
- repeating cycles of increasing and decreasing prices.

The following charts show examples of these four patterns. Each example plots historical prices over time. Also, some charts include a trend line, which is a straight line that connects:

- significant lows of an increasing price series;
- significant highs of a decreasing price series.

Rising Prices

A rising price pattern has a general trend of increasing prices. The chart for Minnesota Mining & Manufacturing (MMM), a conglomerate, shows a long-term rising price pattern with two trend lines. As prices move higher, the short-term tops in price increase. Also, the short-term lows that touch the trend line occur at higher prices. Therefore, the short-term highs and lows move higher for an increasing price pattern.

Figure 7. Rising price pattern with trend lines.

Declining Prices

A declining price pattern is a trend of declining prices. The prices move up and down above the declining trend line. The chart for Hecla Mining (HL), a silver mining company, shows a long-term declining price pattern. The steep increase to $25 is an example of the volatile nature of price changes in silver and gold mining stocks. Also note that as prices decrease the fluctuating short-term peaks become lower and the fluctuating short-term lows become lower. Lower highs and lower lows are characteristic of a decreasing price pattern.

BUY ON THE UPSIDE 91

Figure 8. Declining price pattern with trend lines.

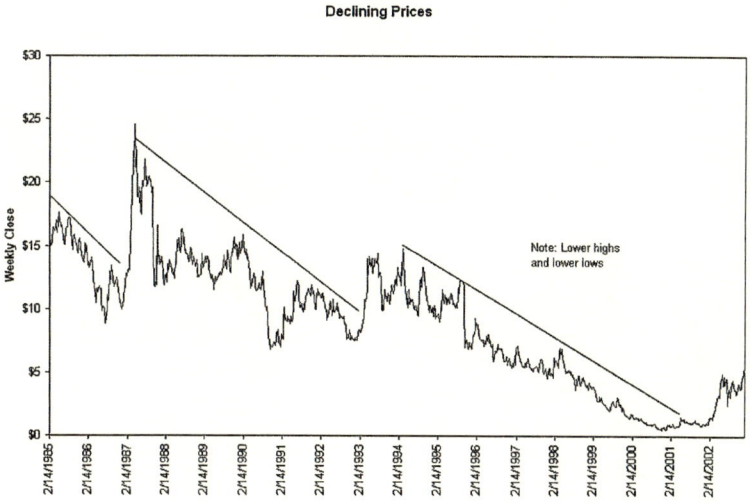

Sideways Prices

A sideways pattern is a trend of unchanging prices. The prices move up and down within two horizontal trend lines which are defined by the high and low prices for the pattern. The horizontal patterns end when prices form a rising or a declining pattern. The chart for Southern Company (SO), a large electric utility, shows a horizontal price pattern that ends when prices form a rising pattern. Notice that prices fluctuate within the upper and lower price bands.

Figure 9. Sideways price pattern with trend line.

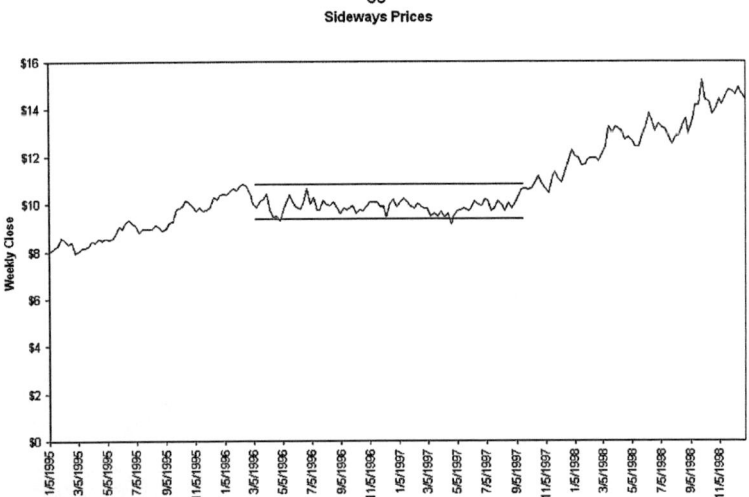

Repeating Cyclical Prices

The next chart shows repeating cycles for Kulicke & Soffa (KLIC). Each of the four cycles has a well-defined upside, a sharp peak, and a downside of prices. This cyclical pattern repeats itself cycle after cycle.

Figure 10. Repeating cycle price pattern.

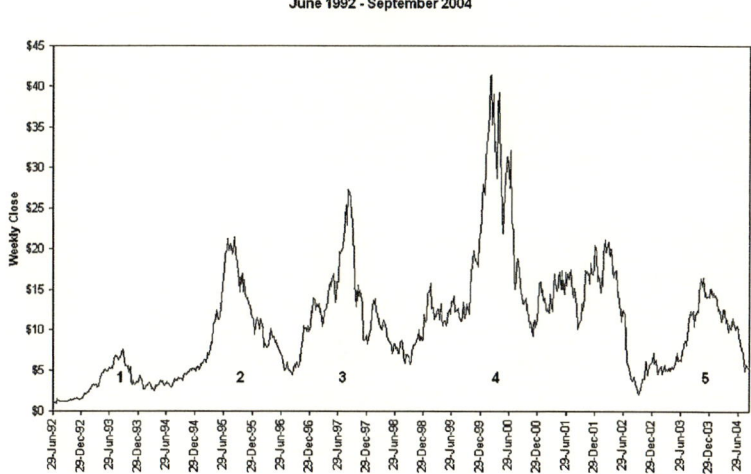

Topping Patterns

Prices do not rise forever. The topping pattern is the end of the rising price pattern. When the topping process is complete, prices fall. Four topping patterns are:

- sharp top;
- double top;
- multiple top head and
- shoulders top.

The following examples show the topping patterns.

Sharp Top

The sharp top of Home Depot (HD), the large home-building supply store, is well defined by a steep and steady price rise. The initial down move from the top is also steep and steady. The sharp top clearly stands out from the prices preceding the sustained up move.

Figure 11. Sharp-top price pattern.

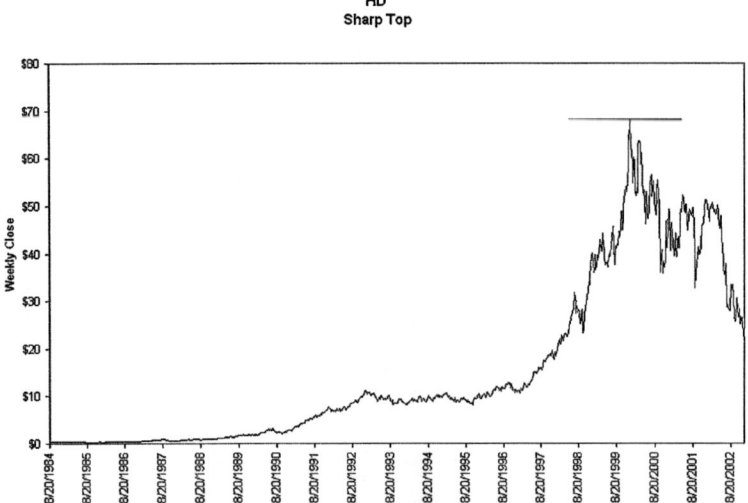

Double Top

A double top has two tops of approximately the same price. Prices rise to a peak, fall, and then rise a second time to the previous high after the second peak prices fall. The chart for Amazom.com (AMZN), an Internet retailer, illustrates the double top.

Figure 12. Double-top price pattern.

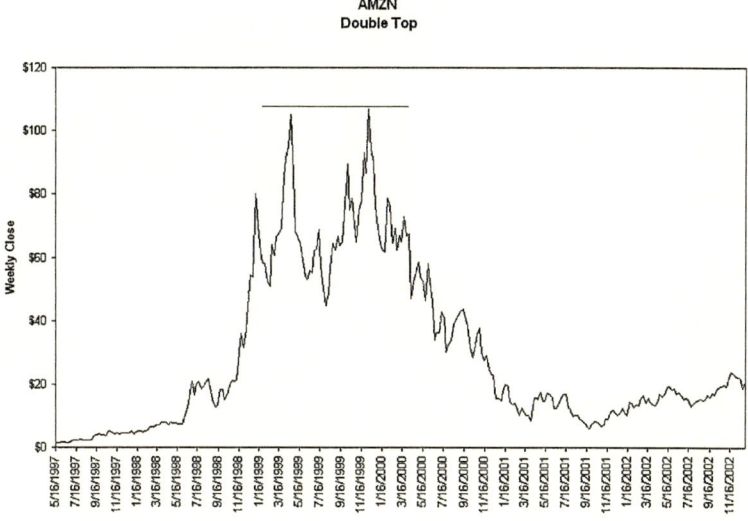

Multiple Top

A multiple top has more than two tops of approximately the same price. The chart for Schering-Plough (SGP), a large pharmaceutical company, shows five tops between $53 and $55.

Figure 13. Multiple-top price pattern.

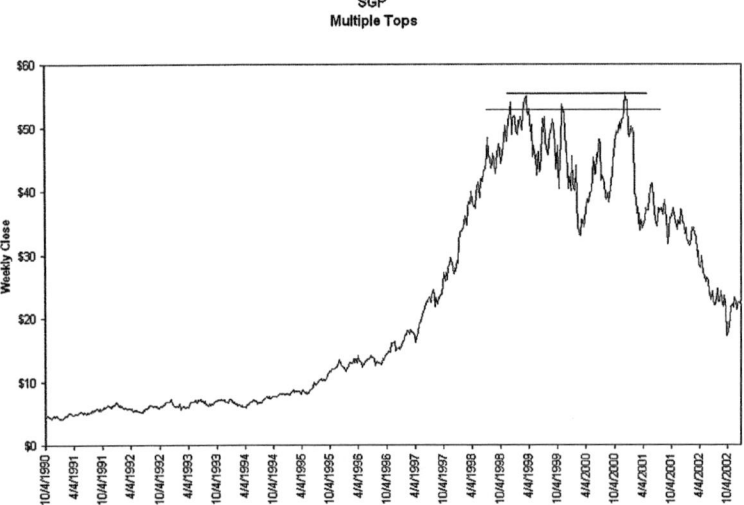

Head and Shoulders Top

A head-and-shoulders top has three components: a temporary top followed by a higher top, which is followed by a lower temporary top. The first rise, top, and decline is called the left shoulder. The second rise, highest top, and decline is the head. The next rise, lower top, and decline is the right shoulder. Prices continue to decline after the right shoulder. The chart for General Electric (GE), the well-known conglomerate, shows a head-and-shoulders-top price pattern.

Figure 14. Head-and-shoulders-top price pattern.

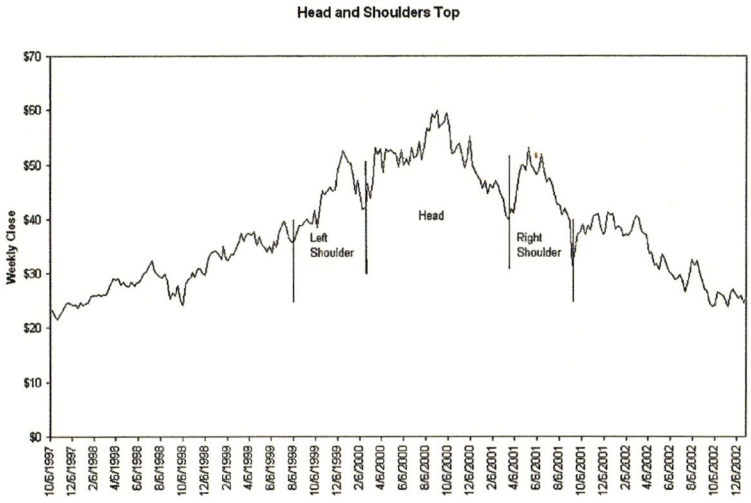

Bottoming Patterns

A bottoming pattern is the end of the declining price pattern. When the bottoming process is complete, prices obviously rise. The bottoming patterns are:

- rounding bottom;
- sharp bottom;
- double bottom;
- multiple bottom.

The following examples show bottoming patterns.

Rounding Bottom

A rounding bottom is formed as prices decline gradually over time. Also, prices move off the bottom price slowly. Therefore, you don't know when the bottom price has occurred until well after the fact. The chart for Placer Dome (PDG), a gold mining stock, illustrates the price movement of a rounding bottom.

Figure 15. Rounding-bottom price pattern.

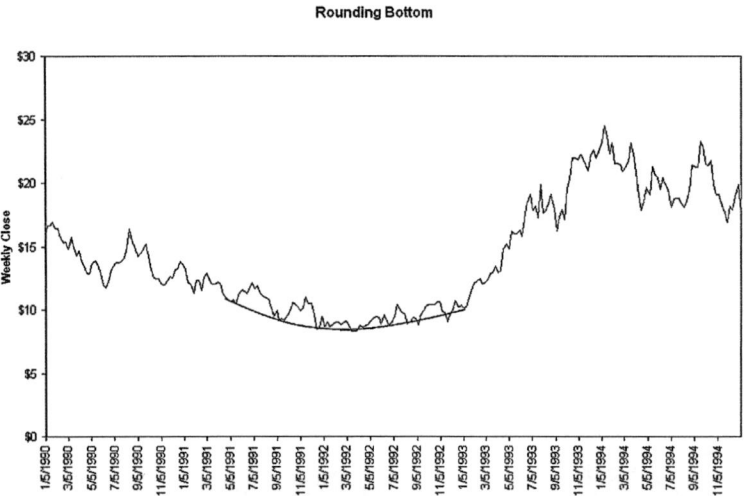

Sharp Bottom

The sharp bottom is a well-defined end of declining prices. After the low price occurs, prices rise steadily. The sharp bottom for Eastman Kodak (EK), a photographic equipment manufacturer, is easily seen in the price chart.

BUY ON THE UPSIDE

Figure 16. Sharp-bottom price pattern.

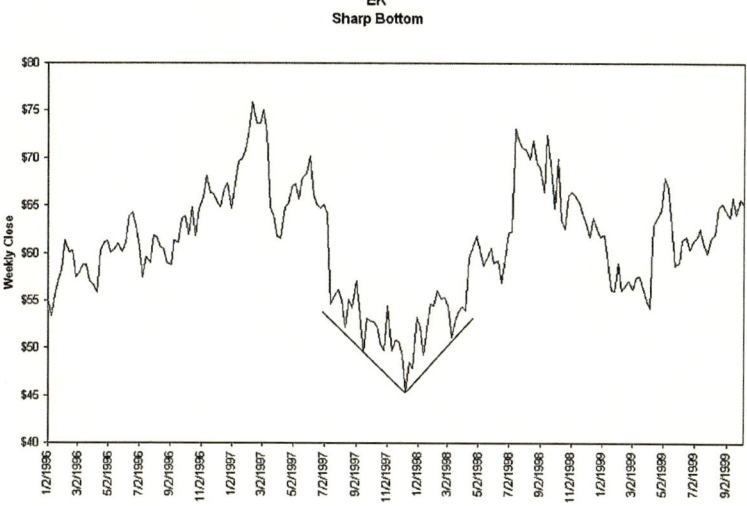

Double Bottom

The double bottom has two lows that share the same values. After the second bottom, prices rise. The chart for Weyerheuser (WY), a forest products firm, illustrates the double bottom.

Figure 17. Double-bottom price pattern.

Multiple Bottom
A multiple bottom consists of more than two low prices that are close in value. Prices rise after the last low price. Diamond Offshore (DO), an oil-drilling company, has three lows at $20.

Figure 18. Multiple-bottom price pattern.

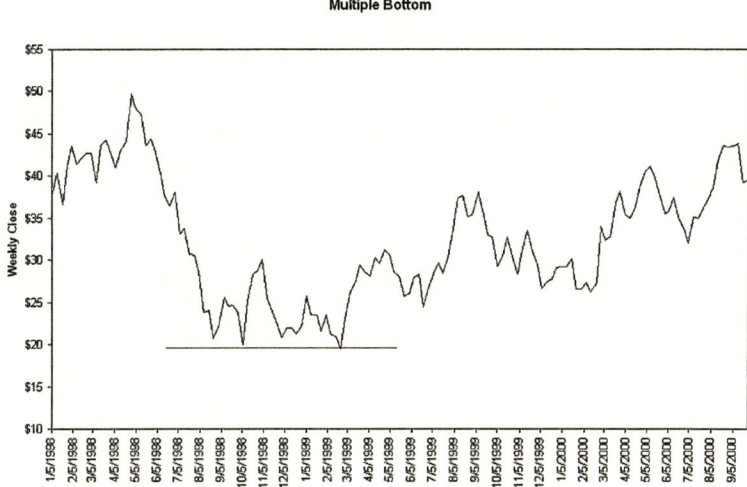

Conclusions and Recommendations

Price charts contain information that helps you know whether you're on the upside, downside, or near a top or bottom. Understanding price patterns will assist you in making well-informed buy-and-sell decisions. Before you buy or sell a stock, study and interpret its price charts. For more on price patterns read *The Visual Investor* by John Murphy.[16]

CHAPTER 6

The Wizard of Oz

Dorothy learned to rely on her own perceptions. You as an investor must learn from your own decisions, both good and bad. Once you are an independent investor you are not in Kansas anymore. Look behind the screen; see the wizard as he really is. Here, in simple and summary form, are the principles you need to follow to insure that you are a confident, focused investor.

Have a Plan

Before you start to invest money in the stock market, you need to develop a long-term savings plan and a long-term investment plan. The plans have different objectives. Your savings are the difference between your income and expenses. A savings plan sets aside money for different purposes, one of which is long-term investing. The savings plan determines how much money you have to invest—all or part of your savings is the input to your investment plan. The investment plan makes the savings grow over time.

The Overlap of Your Investing Experience and the Ups and Downs of the Market

If your investing career coincides with an up trend in stock prices, you have a good chance to make money. You make money simply because more stocks are going up than going down, so you catch the money-making wave when many stocks move up together. In sustained up markets, investors of all stripes make money because buying and selling on the upside is a winner's game. On the other hand if you invest when the market is in a long-term down trend, you probably will have small gains or lose money. No amount of investing skill and experience can fully counteract the negative effects of a multiyear down market. Losing stocks overwhelm winning stocks, so it's very difficult to make money. Buying and selling on the downside is a loser's game.

Reminders:

- If your investing career overlaps an up market, you have a good chance of making money.
- If your investing career overlaps a down market, you have a poor chance of making money.

Make Projections about the Future Direction of Prices

History confirms that stock prices move in up and down. For cyclical stocks the up and down moves occur with some regularity. Broad market averages like the DJIA, S&P 500 and NASDAQ have patterns of multiyear up moves followed by multiyear down moves. You need to know where you are in these cycles because some investing strategies work well in an up trend but do not work in a down trend. Study price patterns of many individual stocks and stock market indices to learn to spot up and down moves. Price charts are visual records of the price action for a stock. A price chart is to an investor what an x-ray is to a physician. With charts, you can make educated guesses where prices are likely to go in the future. Obviously, predicting future prices is a very difficult task but at a minimum you want to be able to say that you think prices are going up, staying flat, or going down. You don't have to know how high or low but you need to estimate the general direction of price movement.

Reminders:

- Know long-term price patterns of market, sector, and individual stocks.
- Look for price bubbles.
- Know how to identify up trends and top formations.
- Know how to identify down trends and bottom formations.
- Estimate the direction of future prices before you make investment decisions.

Understand What Can Go Wrong and Limit Losses

You can make significant money in the market, but you can lose lots of it as well. You can buy the stock of a poorly managed company, buy the stock of a good company but pay too much, buy on the downside, borrow money to buy a stock and then have the stock price collapse, or have a totally unexpected event crush the stock. Bad things happen to investors. Very few, if any, investors are immune to losing money from time to time. For example, you turn the TV on and learn your favorite company is down 60 percent that day because they just announced an unexpected accounting irregularity. No amount of due diligence on your part could have prevented the stock collapse. It just happened.

If the stock accounts for a small percentage of your portfolio, you're unhappy but the financial damage need not be significant. But if the stock is 90 percent of your holdings, your loss is significant. You must learn to guard against situations that can lead to sudden financial pain or long-term ruin.

Before you commit money to an investment, always think about the worst-case scenario. Always ask: "What happens to my financial security if I lose every dollar I put into this investment?" John Bogle, the founder of Vanguard Investments, put it succinctly, "Uncertainty is the possibility that you will lose a lot of money just when you need it most." Reminders:

- Be serious about any investment. It can go against you at unexpected times.
- Understand the consequences of a loss. Can you sustain it?
- Before you make any investment, list the reasons why the investment could go bad. If your list has had no entries, don't invest because you don't understand enough about the investment.
- Limit your losses. If a stock goes bad for whatever reason, don't be afraid to sell it for a loss. Rather than let a small loss turn into a very large loss, sell a stock when it falls a predetermined amount. For example, you could sell a stock if it dropped 20 percent from the purchase price. Determine the sell trigger before the stock starts to fall so that the sell decision is mechanical rather than emotional.

You Have the Final Say

During your investing career, you'll receive lots of advice from friends, family, colleagues, radio and TV, books and magazines, and brokers and money managers. Some of the advice is sound and a lot of it is pure junk. You have to know the difference. Remember that when you make a decision to buy, sell, or hold that it's your financial well being that's at stake. It's your money. Therefore, don't be in a great hurry to part with your money just because another person recommends a stock.

Reminders:

- Make your own decisions.
- Think independently.
- Don't follow the herd unless you can give yourself good reasons to do so.

Avoid the Compulsion to Buy

Investors who lived through the 1982-2000 bull market were conditioned to buy. They bought at almost any price and most were rewarded. The propaganda machine was in high gear and investors responded by pumping trillions of dollars into the stock market. Buying on dips in price often paid off because the market was on the upside for twelve years. Even as the market spiked up and began to fade in 2000, the "Buy Propaganda Machine" said, "It's different this time—keep buying." And people kept buying only to see steep declines in the next few years. Recall the 1929 compulsion to buy which led to money-losing investments for the next twenty-five years. Investors who bought the NASDAQ bubble in 1999 and 2000 will wait years before they break even and during that time inflation will eat away at their investments.

Reminders:

- Serious investing is not a trivial pursuit.
- Beware of the various sales pitches from the "Buy Propaganda Machine."
- Beware of the herd mentality.
- Beware of fad stocks.
- Beware of "It's different this time" advice.
- Ask, "Why shouldn't I buy the stock?"
- You don't have to buy today; the stock will be there tomorrow.

Carefully Select Buy-and-sell Prices

Buying and selling stocks at the right prices determines your financial gains and losses. The art of buying a stock is not to pay too much and the art of selling is not to receive too little. CTM shows you that the percent winning trades on the upside is in your favor but the percent winning trades on the downside is stacked against you. It is very difficult to make money when you buy on the downside. Buy on the upside and never buy on the downside. Use the Price Direction Indicator (PDI) and CTM to identify upside prices and downside prices.

Reminders:

- Read the chart before you buy.
- Read the chart before you sell.
- Buy on the upside after the bottom is well established.
- Don't pay too much. Check for peaks and check price-to-earnings ratio.
- DO NOT buy on the downside. Wait for the bottom to be established. Why pay $40 on the downside and

have the stock go to $20, or worse, have the stock go to $1? Wait for the upside and buy the stock at $40 and have it go to $50.
- Don't buy on dips on the downside.
- Sell at or after peaks.
- Sell to take profits.
- Sell to avoid further losses.
- Sell immediately if you realize you just bought on the downside.
- Use CTM and PDI to identify upsides and downsides.

Diversification Does Not Always Protect You from Losses

Some diversification is good because owning several stocks helps soften the blow if one or two stocks suffer. But too much diversification is counterproductive because owning too many stocks means you'll have losers as well as winners. Diversifying in a single sector—for example, telecommunications—doesn't give much protection because the stocks in that sector are highly correlated, so when one goes down, they all tend to go down. Read the articles in "Sample Portfolios" for examples of stock portfolios.

Reminders:

- If you are good at picking winners, you don't need to own many stocks.
- If you are not good at picking winners, you need to diversify; but as you own more stocks, you may have more losers.
- Owning many stocks in the same sector is not wise diversification.

- A well-diversified portfolio includes stocks that are not highly correlated—they do not all go up and down together.

Dollar-cost Averaging Does Not Always Lead to Profits

When you dollar-cost average, you invest a fixed amount at a regular interval no matter what the stock price. Dollar-cost averaging is a systematic investing method that helps you make money if the stock is in a long-term up trend. However, if the stock goes into a prolonged downturn, dollar-cost averaging will not ensure that you make money. Yes, you buy more shares as the stock prices decreases, but if it keeps going down, your accumulated shares decrease in value. You may end up with a loss. If the stock continues to slide, simply stop buying it and wait until it starts to recover. That way, if the stock is in a very long-term slump you have not committed fresh money on the downside. Reminders:

- Dollar-cost averaging makes money on the long-term upside.
- Dollar-cost averaging may not make money in the long-term downside.

Holding Stocks for a Long Time Does Not Always Ensure Gains

Conventional Wall Street wisdom says to buy and hold stocks to capture long-term gains. The buy-and-hold strategy says to buy stocks and then ride out the ups and downs in prices. Because the long-term price pattern of the broad U.S. stock market has been a long-term up trend, you will be rewarded in due time.

But the individual investor doesn't have an investing career of hundreds of years. Your returns are determined by the price moves for a much briefer period. As such, your returns can be well above or well below the long-term average returns. So long-term average returns for the market based on hundreds of years of performance data have little meaning for individual investors.

The problem with the buy-and-hold approach is twofold. First, if you start your investing career paying high prices or buying at the peak and then enter a multiyear down trend in prices or a period of stagnant prices, you may not break even for years and may never accumulate much profit.

The second problem is you may not live long enough to benefit from the up trend if your investing period coincides with a multiyear period of down prices. However, if you are fortunate to start investing in a period of low prices at the start of a multiyear up trend, you can benefit from the buy-and-hold strategy.
Reminders:

- A long-term buy-and-hold strategy may or may not reward you.
- Long-term performance averages have little meaning to retail investors.
- Prices move up and down over time so your gains move up and down over time.

- Returns for long-term holding periods are more predictable than returns for short-term holding periods.

Dividend Reinvestment Is an Easy Way to Increase Your Returns

When you buy a stock that pays a dividend, you can receive the dividend in cash, or for most stocks, you can reinvest the dividend to buy more shares. Dividend reinvestment is one form of dollar-cost averaging that we strongly recommend. For many investors the cash dividend would be small because you don't own enough shares to receive a large dollar amount. Therefore, you would probably "waste" the small dividend amount. In this case, reinvest the dividends and increase the number of shares you own. If the stock does well, you'll increase your shares without investing any new money. The dividend is a dollar bonus you receive from the original money you invested, so it's not new, out-of-your-pocket money. (Obviously, if you need the dividends for part of your income, you would not reinvest them.)

Reminders:

- Dividend reinvestment is a form of dollar-cost averaging.
- Dividends result from "old money." You don't spend new money to fund dividend reinvestment.
- Dividend reinvestment does not protect you from losing money on the downside.

Read "All about Dividends" for more information on dividends, dividend-paying stocks, and dividend-paying mutual funds.

Buy Index Funds If You Do Not Want to Own Individual Stocks

If you want to participate in the stock market and you don't want to buy individual stocks, you can buy a mutual fund, which is a portfolio of stocks. A fund can be either managed or not managed. A managed fund is run by a professional manger who buys and sells stocks for the fund. Some managed mutual funds return handsome rewards; but unfortunately, many managed funds do not perform better than the benchmark S&P 500, the index for the five hundred largest public corporations in the United States. So you pay commissions and fees to underperform the broad market.

We prefer to buy a nonmanaged fund called an index fund that tracks a selected group of stocks. For example, the Vanguard Index Trust 500 tracks the S&P 500 index. The fund manager simply owns all stocks in the S&P 500. Because the manager does not have to actively decide what stocks to buy and sell, the fund's expenses are very low. High expenses substantially reduce your gains. For example, assume you invest $10,000 and receive a 6 percent return each year for thirty years. If you pay no fees, your total amount is $57, 434.91. If you pay a 1 percent annual fee, your total is $42,484.63; and if you pay a 2 percent annual fee, your total is $31,329.84. These seemingly small amounts dramatically reduce your total return.

Reminders:

- Many actively managed mutual funds do not outperform the market.
- Index funds, with low fees, almost match the index.
- High fees reduce your gain.

Appreciate the Power of Cash

Don't be afraid to hold cash, particularly if you are nervous and uncertain about the future direction of the stock market. Remember a down market is not your friend. You don't have to buy a stock just because it's dropped in price. Even if cash doesn't give you a high return, you're not losing principal and you have the flexibility to scoop up true bargains should they become available. You don't have to be "fully invested in stocks" as the Wall Street professionals often say.

Reminders:

- Cash gives you flexibility.
- In the short term you don't lose money with cash.
- Cash lets you sleep soundly, especially in uncertain times.

Good luck, invest wisely, sleep soundly.

CHAPTER 7

The Fox and the Hedgehog

Sir Isaiah Berlin[17] popularized the fable of the fox and hedgehog by applying it to politicians. He contrasted foxes, who know many tricks and strategies, with the hedgehogs, who have one big idea. He tended to think hedgehogs came out ahead when their idea was right, and disastrously badly when it was wrong, but on the whole, better than foxes, who wasted time on trivia. We think that to be successful in investing, you need to be both hedgehog and fox. Your big idea is why you are investing, your large life goals and your specific objectives. Your foxiness is your employment of a variety of strategies and concepts to achieve your goals, and your flexibility in fitting in with the stock market behavior that your investing life overlaps. Here we present a checklist based on the principles in chapter 6 for your investment program, which is as close to a recipe as we think it is wise to come, given the great variation in investors and goals.

The Checklist
The Big Picture: Where do you want to go in life, and how much time and money do you have to help you get there? Do you have or can you develop an attitude that will enable you to be a serious investor? If you are of ordinary financial means, you probably will have to favor making money over living large to be one. Most successful retail investors are

capable of holding rigorously to a budget so that they can divert some income for investment capital (see the next section). Your investment working capital should be separate from, and come after, an assured place to live, money to cover truly fixed expenses, and cash savings equal to what you would need to live for at least six months if your income dropped suddenly. And remember, this book is just about stocks. There are many other ways to invest.

Assess your resources: What do you own, what are your fixed and discretionary expenses, and what is your income? What size initial investment capital fund can you create? Net worth is the sum of what you own, in total (cash, stocks, bonds, real estate, livestock, everything) minus what you owe (credit card debt, mortgages, car loans, everything you must repay). Your net worth is a useful number and concept, but it doesn't tell you much about what you can or should invest in stocks. For example, you may have a paid-off house worth, say, five hundred thousand dollars, and no other debts. Nevertheless, we would not recommend taking out a mortgage to free money to invest in stocks. Your investment working capital comes after, and is separate from, an assured place to live. You create your capital fund from current income, whether from a job, an inheritance, a tax refund, or other current source. If a tax-sheltered way to accumulate current income for investment is available to you (and it is to most) use it. A regular diversion of current income into an investment fund is the surest way to build it. You can build your investment capital fund and invest at the same time. In any case, it is imperative to first recognize a separate portion of your total resources to use to invest in stocks, and to build and track it systematically.

Set specific objectives for your investment capital fund, for both input and output. The input objectives are usually the sources and amounts of current income you put in the fund monthly or as an initial lump sum or both. The output objectives should be both long and short term. Retirement income is a frequent output goal. How much will you need from your investment capital fund to assure a comfortable retirement in your own terms? Are you building the fund for the education of children or grandchildren, to buy a home, second home, boat, or farm? The key is to estimate how much money you will need and when you will need it. The most empowering thing about creating and recognizing your investment capital fund is the realization that it is yours, your money, and it is there to do your bidding.

The plan you make should be completely explicit. That means that it doesn't include wishful thinking and hand waving. Earlier we described several investing styles. Obviously, this is really a continuum, and you should carefully place yourself on it. If you mostly don't want to be bothered by stock investment decisions but still want the advantages of stock ownership, you could put your investment capital into an index fund or its equivalent in ETFs. Almost every plan should include systematic acquisition of stocks that take advantage of dividend reinvestment. This is a good place to use dollar-cost averaging.

Your decision support system includes all sources of data and advice that support your plan. Your broker and/or stock account is a key component of your system, as is your access to online data. We think that with these two sources of support, you can manage toward almost any set of goals, with almost any size investment capital fund. Expensive newsletters, newspapers, and magazines are sometimes helpful but not necessary, and add to your expenses.

Monitoring against your goals is the most important and most neglected item on this list. At least once a month, check the performance of each component of your portfolio with respect to your specific objectives, and record it. Look at the overall performance of your portfolio as well. If it isn't satisfactory, use your decision support system to find out why.

Supplement the checklist above with frequent visits to *www.buyupside.com* and begin now to become a truly independent investor.

ENDNOTES

1. B. Malkiel, *A Random Walk on Wall Street*.
2. B. Graham, *The Intelligent Investor*. Buffet quote from preface.
3. N. Tales, *Fooled by Randomness*.
4. NASD, number of security dealers.
5. Bureau of Labor Statistics, number of dentists.
6. J. Bogle, "Mutual Fund Industry Assets."
7. *Forbes*, "Criminalizing Capitalism," May 12, 2002.
8. Investment Company Institute, mutual fund annual fees.
9. Eighty-five percent of mutual funds do worse than the S&P 500.
10. Siegal, historical returns of stock market are 6-8 percent.
11. Yahoo Finance, upgrades and downgrades, KLIC.
12. Bureau of Labor Statistics, securities dealers job description.
13. *Money*, "Investor Experiences," September 2002.
14. *Moneypaper*, advice on buying stocks.
15. W. Buffet, *Focus Investing*.
16. J. Murphy, *The Visual Investor*.
17. I. Berlin, *Fox and Hedgehog*.

Web Site Companion to This Book

www.buyupside.com

INDEX

A
American Express 75

B
Berlin, Isaiah 114
Bogle, John 28, 105
broker 19, 33, 37
   securities representatives 26
buy on the upside 24, 50
buy-and-hold strategy 29, 30, 65, 68, 109

C
cash 25
   dividends 46
   rules for saving money 41
   savings plan 64
   value of holding 113
Complete Trading Model 12, 87

D
decision support system 8, 17, 86
   DSS approach 22
dividends 13
   dividend reinvestment 72, 111
      setting up your own account 78
dollar-cost averaging 47, 79, 109
DPL Inc. 75
Duke Realty 75

E
exchange-traded fund 45

F
Fooled by Randomness 23

H
Howard, Richard 11
humint 20
hypothesis 22

I
Individual Retirement Account
   choosing a financial institution 44
   fees 45
inflation 42
investment 9
   automatic transfer 46
   buy high, sell low 32
   checklist for sound investment 117
   downgrade recommendations 32
   fundamental analysis 10, 12
   long term, definition of 30
   principles 102
   qualities for success 17
   roadmap to profitable investing 40
   styles 64

technical analysis 10
upgrade recommendations 32
when to buy, when to sell 52
investor
   aggressive investor,
      definition of 51
   commitment 34
   confidence 35
   fully invested 49
   gut feeling 35

K
Kulicke & Soffa 32

M
Malkiel, Burton 9
market capitalization 13. *See also* See also stock
mutual funds 28
   charges 28
   index fund 44
   index funds 112
   managed funds 49, 84
   taxes 85

N
National Association of Securities Dealers 26
Nikkei 225 71

P
Pfizer 80
portfolios 30
   diversification 81, 108
   focused 82
   market index 67
Price Direction Indicator 12, 87

R
Random Walk on Wall Street, A 9
random-walk notion 9
retail client 19
retail investor 8, 27
retirement 65
Roth Individual Retirement Account 43

S
SPY 45
Standard & Poors 500 42
stock 12
   cyclical stocks 87
   fundamental analysis 86
   kinds of 51
   price patterns 101
   shares outstanding 13
   splitting 13
   technical analysis 86
stock funds 28

T
three-pile plan 18
trading 19
   day trader 20

V
Vanguard 500 Index Fund 74
Vanguard 500 Index Trust Investor Shares 45

W
Wall Street Buy Machine 16, 26, 31
Wilshire 5000 28
Wrigley 76